WHAT I LEARNED FROM MY MILLIONAIRE MENTOR

And How This Knowledge Can Launch
Anyone On a Path to Making Millions

J.T. LAWSON

ISBN 979-8-218-28956-0

Copyright © 2023 by J.T. Lawson

Clay Clark Publishing

Published by Clay Clark Publishing
1100 Suite #100 Riverwalk Terrace
Jenks, OK 74037

Printed in the United States of America

CONTENTS

CONTENTS

PREFACE BY CLAY CLARK

I first met J.T. Lawson because he was on employee for one of my clients. I quickly grew to respect J.T. as a diligent human who was focused on over-delivering and becoming the best version of himself possible. I developed a desire to mentor J.T. when he had consistently demonstrated the habit of over-delivering in my workplace. While working for one of my clients (ScoreBBall.com), J.T. expressed an interest in joining our team during the 7am - 2pm work hours that were before his regularly scheduled hours at Score BBall. During his time on my payroll he has always done what he said he was going to do while working with a vivacious and alacrity that is rare in the workplace. I'm honored to be considered a mentor to J.T. Despite growing up poor, making money has always been easy to me, and I get a great joy out of teaching people how to become super successful because no one needs a mentor to learn how to become mediocre.

INTRODUCTION
Who is my millionaire mentor?

"I am the self-proclaimed most humble man on the planet." (This is classic Clay Clark humor).

Clay Clark

"Somehow I can't believe that there are any heights that can't be scaled by a man who knows the secrets of making dreams come true. This special secret, it seems to me, can be summarized in four Cs. They are curiosity, confidence, courage, and consistency, and the greatest of all is confidence. When you believe in a thing, believe in it all the way, implicitly and unquestionably."

Walt Disney

(An American entrepreneur, animator, voice actor and film producer. A pioneer of the American animation industry, he introduced several developments in the production of cartoons. As a film producer, Disney holds the record for most Academy Awards earned by an individual, having won twenty-two Oscars from 59 nominations.)

The first time I stepped into Clay Clark's office, I noticed how important your environment is. He had quotes written on every wall from various successful people, including Clay himself. Throughout this book, I will have some of those quotes in each chapter. I have had a lot of mentors in my life: great mentors and terrible mentors. Some mentors were coaches, some were mentors from books, some were people I actually built relationships with. Some of the best advice I have ever gotten was from a high school girlfriend's grandpa. In high school, I had a financial peace class where we went over one of Dave Ramsey's workbooks and videos. Dave Ramsey is a very successful financial coach, radio host, author, and businessman. In those workbooks and videos, Ramsey had talked about why credit cards were bad and why you should never even use them; You should cut them up with scissors. I went and told my ex's grandpa this and he disagreed with that statement. However, he agreed with some of the other things Ramsey talked about. He gave me advice that I always fall back on: "No one you meet is going to know all the answers. When someone gives you advice, it doesn't matter if you agree or not. You need to look them in the eye and say 'Yes sir' or 'Yes ma'am'. Afterword, you can decide if its advice worth listening to. You take bits of advice from everyone, implement the advice you want, then it will mold you into who you want to be. "I've been using that advice ever since. Even if I don't like the person or at the moment I disagree with their advice. I either ask follow up questions to understand more or I simply say "Yes sir" or "Yes ma'am." Then I decide later if I want to use their advice. I have also learned it is not worth arguing with people even if you fully disagree. You are not going to change someone's mind who is giving you advice. Truth is I now disagree with a lot of what Dave Ramsey says, but I still agree with some of his advice.

> "We buy things we don't need with money we don't have to impress people we don't like."

Dave Ramsey

(Bestselling author, national radio talk show host, and financial expert)

When I met Clay Clark for the first time I disagreed with a lot of what he was saying. Then I realized it was because I didn't actually know what I was talking about. I'll get into my first interaction with Clay Clark in a later chapter. I have found super successful people have two things in common: A magnificent obsession with achieving success and they are all authentically themselves. That held true for Clay Clark as well. Most people don't understand him, or they think he works too hard. They hear that he wakes up everyday at 3am and thinks he is just a freak who doesn't need sleep. They say his wealth was just a gift that was given to him and he didn't have to work for it. However, they see what he has and they say "must be nice" instead of saying "to have what others have you must be willing to do what they did." So this is some of what Clay has done, and next, I'll tell you what he had to sacrifice to get it.

- Clayton Thomas Clark, Clay Clark (born November 5th 1980) is an American entrepreneur, podcaster, author and public speaker.

CAREER:

- Clay Clark started his career by founding DJ Connection (DJConnection.com) out of his Oral Roberts University dorm room in 1999.

- Between 1999 and 2022 Clay Clark has written 19 books, has founded, co-founded or partnered with: Elephant In The Room Men's Grooming Lounge, Epic Photos, Fears and Clark Commercial Estate, Make Your Life Epic LLC, The ReAwaken America Tour, The Tulsa Bridal Association Bridal Show, Tip Top K9 Franchising, Thrive15.com, etc.

- Clark is the co-host of iTunes top 10 business podcast "Thrivetime Show" with his partner Dr. Robert Zoellner where they teach practical business steps to entrpreneurs looking to start or grow a business and they also interview other top entrpreneuers including Seth Godin, David Robinson, John Lee Dumas, Bruce Clay, Zach O'Malley Greenburg, Tom Peters, Rashad Jennings, Ben Shapiro, Justin Forsett, Gretchen Rubin, and more.

  (https://itunes.apple.com/us/podcast/thrivetime-show-business-school-without-the-bs/id1076405618?mt=2)

AWARDS AND RECOGNITION

- In 2002, Clark was named by the Tulsa Metro Chamber of Commerce as the Young Entrepreneur of the Year.

- In February of 2007, Clark was named by the United State Small Business Administration as the Young Entrepreneur of the Year for the State of Oklahoma.

- Clay and his companies have been seen on Entrepreneur magazine, Forbes, Fast Company, The Washington Post, also a member of the Forbes Coaches Council

  (https://www.forbes.com/sites/ forbescoachescouncil/people/clayclark/)

- Clark co-founded The Elephant In The Room Men's Grooming Lounge (EITRLounge.com) in 2012.

- Clark founded Thrive15, an online video-based education platform for entrepreneurs in 2014

  (https://www.amazon.com/Clay-Clark/e/B004M6F5T4/ ref=sr_ntt_srch_lnk_1?qid=1538662443&sr=8-1)

AUTHOR

- Clark is the author of 19 books. This is a list of his books that he has written as of 2022 which can all be found at https://store.thrivetimeshow.com/

 Start Here: The World's Best Business Growth & Consulting Book: Business Growth Strategies from The World's Best Business Coach

 Fear Unmasked 2.0

 Boom: The Business Coach Playbook: The 13 Proven Steps to Business Success

 Fear Unmasked

 How to Repel Friends and Not Influence People

 THRIVE: How to Take Control of Your Destiny and Move Beyond Surviving... Now!

 Jackassery: Unfiltered Entrepreneurship

 The Art of Getting Things Done

 Don't Let Your Employees Hold You Hostage

 Search Engine Domination: The Proven Plan, Best Practice Processes + Super Moves to Make Millions with Online Marketing

 Podcast Domination 101: The Process and Path to Podcast Success Paperback – February 5, 2020

 Trade-Ups: How to Gain Traction in a World of Endless Digital Distractions

Dragon Energy: The Mindset Kanye, Trump and You Need to Succeed

 Will Not Work for Food – 9 Big Ideas for Effectively Managing Your Business in an Increasingly Dumb, Distracted & Dishonest America

 The Wheel of Wealth – An Entrepreneur's Action Guide by Clark, Clay

 The F6 Journal

 The Great Reset Versus The Great Awakening

 A Millionaire'$ Guide | How To Become Sustainably Rich - A Step-By-Step Guide to Building a Successful, Money-Generating, and Time-Freedom Creating Business

- Clay Clark hosts a daily radio show and podcast with his partner Dr. Robert Zoellner where they teach the steps they took to grow 13 multi-million dollar businesses. They teach practical and actionable steps to grow a business and combine humor in a entertaining way. They also have interviewed highly successful people including

 Sharon Lechter

 Robert Kiyosaki

 John Stockton

 Seth Godin

 David Robinson

 John Lee Dumas

 Dan Heath

 Muggsy Bogues

 Michael Levine

 Lee Cockerell

Jonah Berger

Zack O'Malley Greenburg

Rashad Jennings

Jim Stovall

Ben Shapiro

Adam Berke

Bruce Clay

Tom Peters

John Jantsch

Dionne Phillips

Jerry Vass

Justin Forsett

Ken Auletta

Gretchen Rubin

Michael Corbett

Eric Trump

Mike Lindell

◇ See additional guests at Thrivetimeshow.com

PERSONAL LIFE

Clay is married to his wife of 17 years, Vanessa Clark and together they have 5 kids, 42 chickens, 9 cats, and 2 turkeys.

THROUGHOUT CLAY CLARK'S CAREER HE HAS BEEN FEATURED IN COUNTESS PUBLICATIONS, INCLUDING:

◇ https://www.tulsaworld.com/business/tulsabusiness/business_news/introducing-elephant-in-the-room-men-s-grooming-lounge/article_c56ca539-df0f-54da-862f-2f98ffdbof65.html

◇ https://www.tulsaworld.com/business/business-viewpoint/business-viewpoint-with-clay-clark-of-thrive-what-i-ve/article_b0a17d01-7329-5749-ad95-a213c8e7f-f2e.html

◇ https://pando.com/2014/06/20/thrive15-aims-to-be-the-khan-academy-for-small-businesses-but-can-the-middle-america-site-teach-valley-style-methods/

◇ https://www.tulsaworld.com/business/business-viewpoint/business-viewpoint-with-clay-clark-the-pain-and-gain-of/article_921d51b7-b3f7-53a6-b290-61363d597dco.html

◇ https://www.tulsaworld.com/business/businessviewpoint/clay-clark-success-formula-works-for-entrepreneurs/article_dce4a33d-9ae4-5a0e-bb38-faf-47744cad4.html

◇ http://www.tulsapeople.com/Tulsa-People/May-2014/Five-questions-Clay-Clark/

◇ https://smallbusiness.yahoo.com/advisor/blogs/profit-minded/clay-clark-wants-to-help-entrepreneurs-thrive-205802462.html

- https://www.forbes.com/sites/danschaw-bel/2014/01/22/david-robinson-his-voyage-from-the-nba-to-venture-capi-tal/#4935090665a3

- https://www.forbes.com/sites/forbescoachescoun-cil/2017/09/18/seven-steps-for-scaling-your-busi-ness-most-efficient-ly/#20356de13b21

- https://www.forbes.com/sites/forbescoachescoun-cil/2017/05/26/when-most-people-get-distracted-great-leaders-do-this-in-stead/#c25459451aee

- https://www.forbes.com/sites/forbescoachescoun-cil/2018/08/01/why-most-business-coaching-is-a-waste-of-time/#6f959d0b631c

What you just read are some of the things Clay has achieved. The world looks at people like Clay who now have the time and financial freedom to do whatever they want and think to themselves "That must be nice."

I think to myself, "What did they have to do to get there?" Most people think that you luck into stuff like this.

"I'm a Great Believer in Luck. The Harder I Work, the More Luck I Have"

Thomas Jefferson

(Thomas Jefferson was an American statesman, diplomat, lawyer, architect, philosopher, and Founding Father who served as the third president of the United States from 1801 to 1809.)

I know this to be true; to have what others have, you must be willing to do what they did. Not to be mistaken with what they currently do. What they currently do isn't what got them to this point. So when I look at my mentors I don't think, "How did they get so lucky?" Instead I have a burning desire to understand them and what they did to get there. The more famous people I meet, the more I realize they aren't that impressive; they are still human. With Clay I am truly impressed by his relentless nonstop motor and unwavering discipline. It's what I strive for.

A few quotes that changed Clay Clark's life include:

"A goal is a dream with a deadline."

Napoleon Hill

"Action is the real measure of intelligence."

Napoleon Hill

"Success is a choice."

Napoleon Hill

"The fear of the Lord is the beginning of knowledge; but fools despise wisdom and instruction."

Proverbs 1:7

"He that walketh with wise men shall be wise: but a companion of fools shall be destroyed.

Proverbs 13:20

CHAPTER 1
MY PROMISE TO YOU

"Inspiration is the reward. Inaction is
the giant, and action is the sword."

 Clay Clark ....

(Founder of Thrive15.com and former U.S. Small Business
Administration Entrepreneur of the Year)

"But if someone doesn't provide for
their own family, and especially for
a member of their household, they
have denied the faith. They are worse
than those who have no faith."

1 Timothy 5:8

"And whatsoever ye do, do it heartily,
as to the Lord, and not unto men;
Knowing that of the Lord ye shall
receive the reward of the inheritance:
for ye serve the Lord Christ."

Colossians 3:23-24

In the fall of 2013 I was failing all my college classes
because I stopped going to class. I then realized I couldn't
afford to go to a different college so I returned to working
at the bowling alley where I was making $8.50 an hour
after I had two raises. I attended a school across the street

from my best friend's college because I did not have the grades to be accepted into his college. In the fall of 2014 I had my GPA up to a 2.1 from a 1.8 the previous year. I remembered that I still owed $4,000 to the school before I could go back the next semester. Therefore I did the logical thing at the time and I joined the military to help pay for school. I joined the National Guard to be exact. That way, I could still go to school and party, but I could have it paid for because that was my mindset back then. I went to basic training in Fort Benning, Georgia in January 2015.

Fast forward 3 months we are doing a 4 day FTX (Field Training Exercise). We were being briefed on the mission and what we were supposed to be doing. Our Drill Sergeant tells us the objective and then adds "Does everyone see this tree?" As he points to a tree that is burnt and almost falling over.

"Don't fucking touch it. It's a part of my beautiful forest here and it will stand forever." Then we start digging our foxholes with our E-Tool, which is a 4 foot long collapsible shovel. I take the first shift while my battle buddy pulls security. Eventually we switch. I started pulling security, meaning I'm laying down behind my M249 Squad Automatic Weapon, looking for fake bad guys, which I know during this point of the exercise they aren't actually coming. The sun is absolutely cooking me, but once you accept the sweat puddle under you it starts to feel nice.

I start daydreaming about what it will be like when I get back to school and see my girlfriend and friends. Then my battle buddy starts throwing dirt on me. I realized I had fallen asleep. Nonetheless, it was hot. I was tired and I didn't care, so I ignored it and went back to sleep. I feel more dirt being thrown on me and I say, "Bro fucking stop." This time I feel the dirt hit the back of my helmet. Now I'm pissed and I turn around and say "Bro what the hell is your...yes Drill Sergeant."

My Drill Sergeant is standing there, E-Tool in hand, not smiling. He says, "Lawson here cares more about sleep than the lives of his battle-buddies" I replied while terrified,' 'No Drill Sergeant. "Are you fucking calling me a liar private?" Trying to save face I reply "sorry Drill Sergeant" The Drill Sergeant erupts "Oh so you not only fell asleep and got your whole platoon killed but you also think I'm a sorry Drill Sergeant." I'm trapped in his game and no reply will work so I decide not to respond. He then throws the shovel down and leaves. I got off easy with that one.

A couple hours later and no one was around other than me, a couple people and that tree that was supposed to stand forever. I look around and then impulsively sprint to the tree, jump in the air, and two leg drop kick it. I connected perfectly, then I fell and hit the ground. I looked up at the tree, it didn't fall. My battle buddy said, " Lawson,

what the fuck are you doing? Do you want to get smoked for the rest of the day?" Getting smoked meant the Drill Sergeant made you do physical exercises until you were physically drained. I honestly didn't mind getting smoked. I enjoyed the physical punishment. I ignored him. The impulse of randomly kicking the tree was gone. But the feeling of failure that the tree was still standing was over me like a dark cloud.

I started rocking the tree back and forth, and all of a sudden it snapped and fell down. I truly don't know what I was expecting but I definitely wasn't expecting it to be that damn loud. Then the age out question came up: if a tree falls in the woods, and there isn't a Drill Sergeant around, does it actually make a noise? I sprinted back to my foxhole and jumped in. Shortly after that, I found the answer to the question. The answer is a resounding yes. Our Drill Sergeant comes over and says "Who the hell knocked over my tree?" There was total silence.

He said, "Either everyone gets smoked or one person gets smoked." Immediately someone shouted, "It was Lawson Drill Sergeant!" I was called over, chewed out, and smoked.

Later that night the Drill Sergeant yells, "Alright Charlie Platoon, we are now tactical. All lights off and no one makes a noise." The issue with this is I was on the other side of the camp and didn't hear him. We were about to shoot blanks during an exercise and I had lost my ear pro. Ear pro is just ear protection, normally ear plugs or something similar. I was frantically searching because I was scared my ear drums would burst if I started firing off rounds with the .249. I turn around and yell, "Does anyone have extra ear pro?" The Drill Sergeant yells, "Lawson get the fuck over here!" I yell back, "Yes Drill Sergeant!" And sprint over. Keep in mind, I didn't hear him yell not to make a noise. So I'm running over, and I'm genuinely thinking he has ear pro for me and is helping me out. I sprint over to him, and he looks pissed. I was confused, but honestly he always looked pissed.

I wasn't too worried about it. He proceeded to chew me out for about 5 straight minutes. Now you might be saying, "5 minutes isn't that long." But, 5 straight minutes of someone yelling is a long time. To sum up our one sided conversation, he basically said that I fucked up 3 times today. One more fuck-up and he is kicking me out of his army because I'm not ready to soldier up, and he wouldn't want to fight beside me in war, and how I was a shit bag and on and on. Now, I learned something from being with one of my past girlfriends—If someone is mad at me and I shut off all emotion and show they didn't get to me. It normally turns the argument back around on them and they get more pissed. I tried this tactic with my Drill Sergeant. It seemed to be working, because he just kept getting more and more pissed. He eventually sent me back to my foxhole. While

I was walking back to my foxhole, I thought to myself, "I don't want these other guys thinking he got to me. Stand up straight and make no facial expression. Oh and it will probably be a good idea to whistle to yourself. I mean you are like 50 yards away. No way the Drill Sergeant hears me." So then I started whistling to myself very quietly. In the distance I hear, "Who the absolute fuck is whistling?!"

I turn to my right and see my friend Locklear in the foxhole. I whisper, "Bro please, please, please take the blame for this. Please. I'll pay you." Now this is supposed to be my best friend in basic training. He looks at me and says, "You're fucked buddy. Not a chance." I then hear the Drill Sergeant yell with more anger now, " WHO. THE FUCK. WHISTLED?!" I realize there is no getting out of this. I yell back, "ME Drill Sergeant!" "Holy fucking shit. Lawson! Come back over here," he yells. I run back over. The Drill Sergeant is calm now and has a smile on his face. He calmly says, "Gather all of your stuff and go back to the ammo checkpoint. You will no longer serve in my army."

For the rest of the 4 day FTX I sit at the ammo checkpoint. While no one talks to me. No one asks me to do anything. I offer to help with other things and all the Drill Sergeants just tell me to go sit back down and shut up. When anyone walks by they just look at me and shake their head. Four straight days of sitting and looking at ammo boxes. Then the FTX ends and we go back to the barracks and a different Drill Sergeant informs me that because I didn't complete the FTX, even if the Drill Sergeant changes his mind, I still can't graduate. They stop including me in any of the training. When they would go out for training they would leave me back at the barracks with the people who were getting medically discharged from the army. To this day I don't know if they were playing mind games or if they just forgot they were kicking me out or didn't want to do the paperwork. Somehow, I ended up graduating basic training.

I'll share more stories like this throughout the book because if Clay Clark, my millionaire mentor can help me become successful, he can help you also.

I'm going to start this book off by being very negative. The truth is if you have read multiple books before this and your life is no different, then let me stop you and tell you this book could be pointless to you. Most likely you're what Clay calls an 'Ask-Hole'. You ask for advice, but never implement it. You're looking for a quick fix, or a secret that the world is hiding from you and only a select few know. You're hoping that someone is going to tell you those secrets and you'll be rich in a month or a year.

Now, if you have read books and tried to implement things and they just did not work, I can work with that. If you've never read a self help book, I can work with that.

HERE ARE SOME FACTS TO MAKE YOUR DAY WORSE

- Fact number 1 - According to Bureau of Labor Statistics 2022 labor report only 6% identify as being self-employed.

  https://www.bls.gov/news.release/pdf/empsit.pdf

- Fact number 2 - 96% of businesses fail according to *Inc Magazine*.

  https://www.inc.com/bill-carmody/why-96-of-businesses-fail-within-10-years.html

Clay broke this down and said, "Imagine we were in a church today with 100 members, and one of the pastors said, 'If you are self-employed, stand up.' So 6 guys would stand up. Then, the pastor says, 'Keep standing if you are successful.' 96% of them would sit down. So you would have one person standing at the end."

- Fact number 3 - 75% of employees admit to stealing from the workplace.

https://www.forbes.com/sites/inywalker/2018/12/28/ your-employees-are-probably-stealing-from-you-here-are- five-ways-to-put-an-end-to-it/?sh=5aaf10193386

- Fact number 4 - According to Inc Magazine 85% of people admit to lying on their resumes.

https://www.inc.com/jt-odonnell/staggering- 85-of-job-applicants-lyeing-on-resumes-.html

Here is some more truth for you: this book is written by someone who isn't impressive at all. I've been slightly above average my whole life. I played college basketball, but I didn't go pro. I set the conference scoring record, but my school is basically the equivalent of a D-3 school, so not impressive. I joined the military but I was in the National Guard. I didn't do anything impressive while enlisted. I never got deployed, I never went to specialty schools. I set a Batallion record for the 2 mile run, but I never got a perfect score on the APFT (Army Physical Fitness Test) because I couldn't do max sit ups.

I wasn't impressive with academics either. In fact, I have had a C- average ever since middle school. I only made a 20 on the ACT. I scored a 16 on the math section (after taking it multiple times) After my first semester in college, I had a 1.8 gpa. I couldn't get into Oklahoma State University, so I had to go to the school literally across the street. It was known for students who weren't smart enough to make it into OSU. When I worked at Walmart, I used to see how long I could go without working. I would hide behind boxes on the shelves and play games on my phone.

You're probably asking yourself why you should choose to learn from this loser. Well, the only thing that has ever been impressive about me is my coachability and my work ethic. When combined with what I learned from Clay Clark, I have now been set on a completely different path. You're learning from Clay Clark, not me.

My promise to you is that if you implement the things in this book and are a diligent doer, people won't understand you. They will say, "You need to enjoy life more" or "Why are you trying to do what Clay and other millionaires do?" They will say things like "You changed," or "Why are you even trying? That's not realistic." But truly, most of the people reading this won't implement anything from this book. The ones that do, will stop after the first two weeks. Most likely, most people will stop the moment they are met with criticism or hit one road block. However, hopefully you're one of the few who decide to make a change so you can reach your full potential, and truly live the life you want and are meant to live.

My goal with this book is to give you tools that you can use to immediately change your life if you act on them. Side note: that does not mean make you rich quick. Now, on my journey of learning and growing, I've been known to give unsolicited advice. That's because, as I'm learning, my first thought is, "I have to teach someone this! Why has everyone not read this book? Why are people not acting on this?" Even people who ask for advice either argue with you while you give them advice or they ask for advice and never implement what you tell them. They would be what Clay refers to as an "ask-hole."

Clay's definition of an ask-hole is, "A person who constantly asks for advice, yet always does the opposite of what you tell them." The reason I'm writing this book is because I genuinely believe that every single person on the planet has the potential to be great at whatever they set their mind to. On the flip side, I also know that most people don't have a work ethic, and even if they do, they aren't coachable and they let their ego get in the way. But I see time and time again that they complain about not knowing the "secret," that the world is out to get them, or there isn't enough time and it takes money to make money, or whatever excuse they have. One of the reasons I'm writing this book is that I truly hate writing, but I know I'll come out better after writing this book.

"If you can think, and speak, and write, you are absolutely deadly. Nothing can get in your way."

 Jordan Peterson

(Jordan B. Peterson is a Canadian clinical psychologist, and best-selling author of "12 Rules for Life.")

All of us have potential, but hardly anyone actually does what's necessary to reach it. Most people don't understand the word "want." There are two different meanings to the word. For example, I "want" to be able to do a 900 like Tony Hawk in X games 5, but I don't "want" to put in the work to actually be able to do it. Obviously, if I could snap my fingers and be able to do it I would. Most people "want" to be rich, but they don't really "want" to be rich. If you could snap your fingers and be rich anyone would, but if you have

 to put in 80 hour or more work weeks and eat Ramen Noodles Soup and move back in with your parents to save money you won't do it. I won't promise you an unlimited supply of money or that there is a magical investment that will all of a sudden make you rich. My goal of this book is to tell you about the interactions I've had with Clay Clark and others around him, and share the practical tools and super moves they taught me which have changed my life forever. I also want to talk a little bit about the book mentors I've learned from. However, if you want to try out a get rich quick scheme, I have two old friends of mine who asked me to join their pyramid scheme. I'd be

happy to send you their information. If you want to learn something that will actually work,my promise is that at first you're not going to enjoy implementing the ideas in this book. A few of the most important ones you'll think are not that important and it's super boring. But if you do implement these super moves, they will change your life. If you do, you won't understand how you made it through life without it. That's the first huge thing I learned from Clay: the best way to learn is by doing stuff you hate, failing, and having mentors. There is no growth in comfortability.

> "Most of the population refuses to bore down into a subject. They would rather alleviate their boredom."
>
> "The greats bore down while mediocre people struggle with boredom"

 Clay Clark

(Founder of Thrive15.com and former U.S. Small Business Administration Entrepreneur of the Year)

I did not want to write this book. However, what I did want is to become more articulate, continue on my journey of constant growth and learning, and help others grow as well. I believe writing this book, and being a part of Clay's team as a business consultant will help me do so. I have decided to open a business, be a business consultant, book Clay on media shows and podcasts, manage a rental property, run a TipTopK9 dog training franchise, and write a book all at once. This isn't my chance to brag. It's

my chance to explain what most people won't understand when you start implementing things from this book. Here are some things that have been said to me recently:

- "That's too much structure for someone like you, you've never been disciplined, that will last a month tops."

- "Don't you think it's a little much to be doing all at once?"

- "You've changed."

- "You cheated your way through high school and college. How are you going to write a book?"

- "Don't do that stuff unless you're getting paid for it."

- "All the people you look up to are freaks of nature and insane. Don't strive to be like them."

- "What if you get mean feedback from social media about your book?"

- "Don't most businesses fail? Why not go get a job for a good company?"

- "No one is going to want to learn from you."

- "That's not sustainable. You're going to burn out."

Most of these were from friends and family members. I understand why they would say these things to me. When I was in the military I was what they called a "shitbag". I was in the Army National Guard. To those of you who are active duty or retired active duty, yes, I was a 'weekend warrior', and no I'm not bragging about it. I was not disciplined. I was always joking around and trying to get out of anything other than physical fitness. I loved physical fitness. I almost got kicked out of basic training multiple times for being a jackass. Not because I couldn't pass any test, but because I wasn't coachable and was hanging around other "shitbags". I didn't want to learn, and I didn't want to further my military career. I knew once my contract was up I was getting out. I have massive respect for anyone who has served in the military. At that point in my life however, I wasn't ready to fully soldier up.

Now, to the people who criticized my schooling, yes, I did cheat a lot in school. There has never been a class in middle school, high school, or the five different colleges I went to that I did not cheat to pass. I used to cheat so much and was so good at it that the only time I got caught cheating was because I forgot I was cheating. In 11th grade, at Summit Christian Academy, I had a Spanish test. I wrote down all the words and answers I needed to pass the test on index cards. Through the process of writing it all down on the index cards, I actually learned Spanish. (Shocking, I know). I had the index cards out on my desk, started taking the test, and realized I knew all the answers because of the 10 minutes I spent writing down the answers on the cards. I left the cards on the desk next to my paper. The teacher stood up and started walking towards me. I didn't think anything of it because I wasn't cheating. She walked over and saw an index card on my desk. I'll be honest, trying to explain that I had a tool to cheat, but was not actually using it was very hard. So I ended up making a zero on the only test I didn't actually cheat on.

One more example was I had a final in one of my college classes that I had to pass or I would fail the class for the semester. So at 3 a.m., I broke into the school, broke into the teachers office, found the final with all the answers on it, and took pictures of it. Then, the next day before the final, I wrote all the answers on my thighs so that I could pull my shorts up during the test and look at the answers. Yet here I am, writing a book.

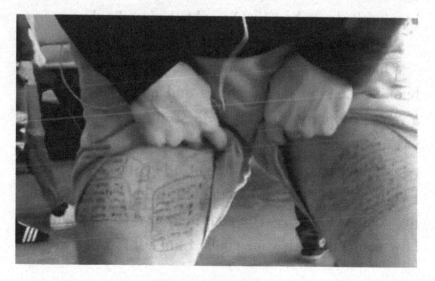

Oh, and here's one more example. I'm actually kind of proud of this one. However, this is in no way a suggestion, advice, or a super move. My freshman year of college I went to a school in Miami, Oklahoma. Long story short, my girlfriend at the time cheated on me and we had 5 classes together, so I stopped going to class the whole semester. I finished the semester with like a 1.8 gpa. The only reason I got a 1.8 and not much lower is because I went to my history final after not going to class all year. I literally had to ask for directions to where the classroom was for the final. I walked in late and sat down. The teachers came and gave me the exam. I acted like I was actually taking the test for about 20 minutes. Then I pulled a $5 bill out of my pocket and taped it on the last page of the final. Under it, I wrote: President Lincoln says I get a D in the class. The professor ended up passing me with a D in the class. Once again, this is not a super move. I'm just telling you this because it shows how bad I used to be in school.

Opening a business, being a business consultant, booking Clay on media shows and podcasts, managing a rental property, running a dog training franchise, and writing a book all at once is a lot to be doing for most people, but compared to Clay or other successful people I know, it's not a lot. The goal of this book isn't to make my goals your goals. The goal is to give you insight into how you can reach your goals. I am 100% okay without having a social life for the next 8 years. I've made that commitment to myself that for the next 8 years I'm going to grind my ass off and implement everything in this book until I've reached the goals I've set for myself. I have an 8 year goal at the time of writing this book because in 8 years I'll be 35. My current goal is to own 2 businesses, bring in $250,000 a year from passive income, own 5 different rental properties, own a ranch, and write two books.

At the time of writing this book, I have just opened 1 business. I bring in around $18,000 a year in revenue from my one rental. If you're reading this, I've completed my first book. Now you can look at this one of two ways. Way number 1 is: that's a daunting set of goals. It is, and if I hadn't learned from Clay Clark and other mentors, I wouldn't have been able to reach any of these goals, let alone be able to think these goals are possible. The second way you can look at it is this: I had none of this before I started working for Clay. Not an exaggeration. I started working for Clay in February of 2021 and I was making $0 in passive income. I had just learned what passive income meant.

Truthfully, I didn't know the concept of passive income was a thing. I was living at home with my parents, with no rental properties, no businesses, and no books written. In 2020, I made $24,389.00 for the whole year. My current goal at that time was to go use my extra year of eligibility and take classes like underwater basket weaving so I was eligible for my last year of college basketball. I didn't need any more credits to graduate, so in order to be eligible I needed to take 1 class per semester. I was going to go back just for basketball. The plan was to go to a pro-placement program in Spain to play basketball professionally. The only reason I wanted to do this was so I could travel the world. Don't get me wrong, I love basketball, but I thought the only way I'd be able to travel the world is if I did it playing professionally. That's the main reason I wanted to play overseas.

You don't know what you don't know. When I met Clay Clark, he shattered everything I thought I knew. It felt like I was in a room that was made of all windows and glass and everything was blacked out. Each time I would hear Clay speak, it would break a window open and I'd start to see into the world of the wealthy. Once a couple windows were broken, I start to realize I've been in a box (or prison).

I started thinking to myself, "What the hell? Why was I not told this earlier? Why does everyone not know this?" My whole life I thought you had to be a movie star, a pro athlete, a drug dealer, a music artist, inherit money, or invent something to have copious amounts of money.

I was in college for about 6 years learning about business, and yet none of the stuff they talked about is what Clay uses in his business practices. College taught about S.W.O.T analysis, and making power points and how to be more culturally inclusive.

If you're reading this and you have a misconception of thinking you have to be smart to reach financial freedom and time freedom, don't fear because I myself am a jackass and Clay says all the time he used to be a jackass. There are a couple limitations you may have put on yourself that I want to shatter in this book. Some of these limitations might include:

◇ Not enough time

◇ What if I'm too old?

◇ What if I fail ?

◇ What if people don't understand my choices?

◇ I don't have money and it takes money to make money.

◇ What will other people think about these changes?

◇ If I change too much, people might not like me.

◇ What if I'm not smart enough?

First let me cover the, "What if I fail?," fear really quick. I realize what I'm about to say is corny, but it's worth thinking about for sure. What if you don't try? Genuinely think about it for a second. You only get one life, why play it safe? Why would you spend all your life working a job you hate, to buy stuff you can't afford, to impress people you don't know? Yes, Gary Vaynerchuk said that first. In 10 years you're going to be 10 years older if you try or not. You owe it to yourself and the people around you to at least try to reach your dreams. If you fail, at least you can look back on your life and say that you actually tried. This is a perspective that I adopted after hearing Denzel Washington's commencement speech at the University of Pennsylvania in 2011. The concept was not originally his, but rather a quote by Les Brown that I discovered after looking it up.

"Imagine if you will, being on your death bed – and standing around your bed – the ghosts of the ideas, the dreams, the abilities, the talents given to you by life. And that you for whatever reason, you never acted on those ideas, you never pursued that dream, you never used those talents, we never saw your leadership, you never used your voice, you never wrote that book. And there they are standing around your bed looking at you with large angry eyes saying 'we came to you, and only you could have given us life! Now we must die with you forever.' The question is – if you die today, what ideas, what dreams, what abilities, what talents, what gifts, would die with you?"

This and some other quotes are taped to the back of my clipboard that I have on me at all times.

As I write this book, I am 28 years old. However, I am aware that by the time I reach 35, there could be countless versions of myself. Therefore, my goal is to become the best version of myself, the one who has committed to waking up at 3:30 am every day for the past seven years and has got after it not just in the gym but in all of my F6 goals (which I will go over into in the next chapter).

I feel my 35-year-old self passionately begging me to maintain an uncommon level of discipline and dedication, to the point where others may view me as crazy. It is through this level of commitment that I can live a life that most people only dream of. If you truly desire the life you want, it is within your reach. I have not encountered anyone who consistently works hard every single day without making excuses, takes action on the things they know they need to do, and seeks guidance when necessary, and has not achieved success.

At the end of each chapter I'm going to have questions for you. Don't treat this book like they taught you in school. I want you to write in this book, highlighting parts that are important to you. Write the answers to the questions in the book.

CHAPTER REVIEW

» Will the criticism from people
you don't know affect you?

» Will the criticism from friends
and family affect you?

» Will doubt from yourself affect you?

» Are you going to let your dreams
and ideas die with you?

» Are you okay with the idea of laying
on your deathbed knowing you
didn't even try to reach your goals?

CHAPTER 2

MONEY IS THE VEHICLE, IT'S NOT THE GOAL

"Design the life you want, or live the life you don't want by default."

Clay Clark

(Founder of Thrive15.com and former U.S. Small Business Administration Entrepreneur of the Year)

"What good will it be for someone to gain the whole world, yet forfeit their soul? Or what can anyone give in exchange for their soul?"

Matthew 16:26

You may have picked this book up because it mentioned learning from a millionaire. You expected this book to be about how to become a millionaire and make copious amounts of cash fast. Now you're pissed at me because of the title of this chapter. Well, hang in there a second. If your goal is only money, you're wrong. I fully understand. I thought the same thing the first time I heard Clay speak at a business conference and he said that. In my head I thought, "whatever, my goal is to be a millionaire, buy my mom a house, and travel the world." Despite that, when he started talking about what he calls the F6 goals, time

The F6 Life
DESIGN THE LIFE YOU WANT OR LIVE THE LIFE YOU DON'T WANT BY DEFAULT.

Psalm 118:24

"This is the day that the Lord has made. We will rejoice and be glad in it."

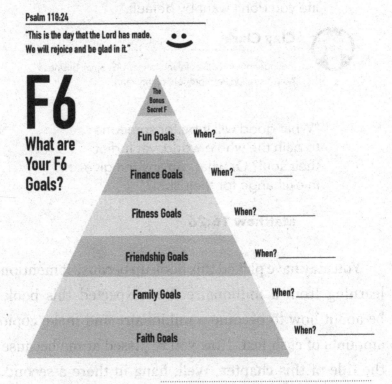

F6

What are Your F6 Goals?

- The Bonus Secret F
- Fun Goals — When?_____
- Finance Goals — When?_____
- Fitness Goals — When?_____
- Friendship Goals — When?_____
- Family Goals — When?_____
- Faith Goals — When?_____

"Control your destiny or someone else will."

JACK WELCH
Former CEO of GE who grew the company by 4,000% during his tenure as CEW

freedom, and financial freedom, he forced the light bulb to click in my head. Clay only had to say it 15 times for it to click. Your goal shouldn't only be money. The goal should be time and financial freedom. If your goal is only to have copious amounts of money and don't care about health or family then hopefully another one of your goals is to get buried in a coffin with all your money in it and no family around. If one of your goals is only to have fun and don't have any financial goals then hopefully your goal is also to live in a van down by the river. After learning from Clay, I now know you have to worry about your F6 goals. The F6 goals are Faith, Family, Friendship, Fitness, Finance, Fun. Here is page 7 from Clay's book "BOOM," it shows the F6 goals pyramid, and no, this is not a pyramid scheme.

I'm sure most of you have been told you need to have a work/life balance and shouldn't work more than 40 hours a week. While the weekend is for going to the lake and getting drunk with friends. If you work weekends and nights you'll burn out. You need to take time to have fun and relax.

Gary Vaynerchuk emphasizes, "Stop working a job you hate, to buy things you can't afford, to impress people whose opinions don't matter." This is true. However, I also know that a bunch of people work jobs they love then complain about having no money. Sometimes working jobs you hate is necessary to earn enough money to be able to fund your startup, business, or hobby.

"We buy things we don't need
with money we don't have to
impress people we don't like".

Dave Ramsey

(David Lawrence Ramsey III is an American radio personality
who offers financial advice. He hosts the nationally syndicated
radio program The Ramsey Show.)

When Clay Clark was working on building his DJ
Connection.com company, he worked at Applebee's,
Direct TV, and Target, all at the same time so he could
afford to grow his company. He and his wife Vanessa lived
in a 1 bedroom apartment, with no air conditioning that
also served as the office. They lived off Ramen noodles,
only had 1 car, and saved every penny they could. This is
what Clay had to do to reach his goals. I'm not saying this
is what you need to do, I'm saying the whole point of the
F6 goals are for you to figure out what your own goals are
and to give yourself a direction in life. Clay says, "design
the life you want or live the life you don't by default." If
you think you will magically drift towards your goals then
surely living in the van down by the river sounds nice to
you. You have to strategically set a target and stay on the
path. Not setting your F6 goals is the equivalent to playing
pin the tail on the donkey, but the donkey is in a different
house. It just doesn't work. The target must be in sight and
you must look at it every single day or you will start to drift.

Let's go through each goal step by step and I'll explain what it is. I'll give you my current goals so you can have an example. At the end of the chapter, I'll tell you what to do so we can get you on your way to time and financial freedom.

At the time of writing this book I currently have this written on my white board for my F6 goals.

- » **FAITH** - Listen to 1 sermon a week. Read 1 chapter of Proverbs every day.

- » **FAMILY** - Visit immediate family 6 times a year. Facetime grandparents once a month.

- » **FRIENDSHIP** - See Jared once a month

- » **FITNESS** - Look like Brad Pitt in Troy. Do whatever my trainer tells me.

- » **FINANCE** - Live off 75% of Clay's paychecks. Save or invest other 25% and all other revenue streams.

- » **FUN** - See Jared (my best friend in Nashville) once a month. Go to the gym.

FAITH GOALS

My current faith goals are to listen to one sermon once a week and to read 1 Chapter of Proverbs a day. There are 31 chapters in Proverbs so I read through Proverbs almost every month. This idea I stole from Clay's good friend Aaron Antis. Also, if I have music playing I want it to be worship music. I care a lot about what goes into my mind everyday so I don't want to listen to most secular music because it's almost all about drugs, sex, cheating, and money.

The only exception to this is when I workout in the mornings in the gym and obviously when I can't control who is playing music. Now you might be reading this and saying, "I don't want to cut secular music out of my life." That's great, these are my goals not yours. "I don't care about my faith goals, I don't want to go to church" or maybe, "once a week isn't enough, I also need to have Bible Study and 1 hour of devotional time a day." Maybe you're thinking, "JT you should be going to church instead of just listening." The good news about what you are thinking is that I don't care. These are my current goals, and they will change one day, but until then this is it. My goal is to help you figure out your goals, not turn my goals into yours. No matter what you set your goals as, someone is going to disagree and say you should be doing more or less in one area.

Establish your faith goals and schedule them.

FAMILY GOALS

I am not married, no kids, and all of my family currently lives a little over 600 miles away. My family goals are to visit my family at least six times a year and to Facetime my grandparents once a month. Your goals might be to take your wife/husband on a date 2 times a week, play catch with your child after school everyday, or have a movie night every Friday. Your goals can be whatever you want them to be. Figure out your family goals and schedule them.

FRIENDSHIP GOALS

Recently I moved to Nashville, Tennessee and the only person I know in Nashville is my friend Jared Minnix, his wife and kids. I was the best man at his wedding back in 2017. So currently my friendship goals are to hang out with him once a month. I'm about to upset a lot of people, but it needs to be said: it is okay to cut friends out of your life. It's also okay to tell a friend you can only see them at certain times on certain days. We will go over this more later in Chapter 7, you can hold off on being offended until then. Your goals might be to designate Friday nights spending time with Billy or designate Monday, Wednesday, and Saturday from 6-8 pm to go play basketball with Timmy. Maybe your goal is to just Facetime your close friend once a week. Once again, that's fantastic. Your goals don't need to be my goals or to be Clay's goals. Establish your friendship goals and schedule it in the calendar.

FITNESS GOALS

Since my college basketball career ended, my goal has been to get as muscular as I can while staying under 12% body fat. Basically to look like Brad Pitt in the movie Troy. Obviously not in the face because I was hit with the ugly stick compared to Brad Pitt. Currently, I'm more of a Brad Pitt in Fight Club which means skinny fit. I used to be very interested in understanding fitness and nutrition. I used to like making my own workout plans and my own nutrition plans. Now I could care less and just want to pay someone to tell me what to do. I told my trainer my goals and he made a workout plan and nutrition plan for me and I do whatever it says. That's what I wanted. I did not want to put any mental energy or time into making the plan. I just want to go into the gym, look at the plan, lift heavy stuff, and leave. However, I have to schedule it in my calendar to go Tue-Wed-Thur-Fri from 4 a.m. - 6 a.m. Sundays are 6 a.m. (the gym doesn't open until 6, very annoying) . Establish your fitness goal and schedule it on the calendar.

FINANCE GOALS

My current goal is to live off 75% of the paychecks I receive from booking Clay Clark for interviews and business coaching. Any money earned from my dog training business or rental properties will be reinvested, whether in real estate or any other venture that produces more revenue. It is important to establish financial goals and schedule them on the calendar.

FUN GOALS

For me my fun goals are easy because I actually enjoy going to the gym. That's currently my only fun goal. Maybe your goals are to be in that underwater basket weaving league every Tuesday night. It might be to be a part of a book club, play board games, or to play golf with your buddies on Saturdays. Maybe your goal is to play a real life game of Frogger in traffic. (Shoutout to the people who remember Frogger.) Make sure your fun goals don't get in the way of other goals. Fun goals are vital so you don't get burnt out, but don't let them interfere with your other goals. For example, if your fun goal is to go get plastered with friends at the club every Saturday night and it's causing you to mess up your faith goals on Sunday morning, I would highly suggest you fix that. Establish your fun goal and schedule it on the calendar.

Clay's goals aren't my goals and they shouldn't be. My goals aren't my best friend's goals and they shouldn't be. You have to figure out your F6 goals, then figure out how much it will cost to make that happen. After that, you have to make a plan of attack on how and when to make that happen which we will go over in the next chapter. You need to have these goals written on a whiteboard or somewhere you can see them every day.

POST CHAPTER QUESTIONS

- » What are your faith goals?
- » What are your family goals?
- » What are your friendship goals?
- » What are your fitness goals?
- » What are your financial goals?
- » What are your fun goals?

CHAPTER 3

MOTIVATION COMES AND GOES, DISCIPLINE LASTS FOREVER

"The greats bore down while most people struggle with boredom"

Clay Clark

(Founder of Thrive15.com and former U.S. Small Business Administration Entrepreneur of the Year)

"You will not magically drift towards your goals. You must make a plan and have your goals in mind every single day. "The number one excuse people use for not getting done what should be done is they did not have time... You either pay now or pay later with just about every decision you make about where and how you spend your time."

Lee Cockerell

(Lee Cockerell is the retired Executive Vice President of the Walt Disney World Resort.)

"The key is not to prioritize what's on your schedule, but to schedule your priorities."

Stephen Covey.

(Stephen Richards Covey was an American educator, author, businessman, and speaker. His most popular book is The 7 Habits of Highly Effective People.)

It was 8 p.m. at Clay's office and Clay came over to me and said, "Do you want to learn how to make copious amounts of money?" With no hesitation I said, "Absolutely." He responded with, "Awesome. Be here at 4 a.m. tomorrow," then grabbed his bag and left. This is an absolute dream for me. The whole reason I wanted to work for Clay Clark was to learn from someone who was super successful at something I wanted to do. I get goosebumps even while writing this.

For me, it was like Christmas Eve and I was 8 years old again, hoping Santa was going to bring me the rabbit named Thumper that I always wanted. (Side note: I did get Thumper and he would bite me anytime I tried to pet him.) I was laying in bed looking at the ceiling trying to guess all the things Clay was going to say to me. Some of my guesses were maybe how to invest money, tell me certain books I need to read, how to find investors, or maybe he was going to teach me how to sell better. Maybe he would talk about stocks, real estate, franchises, or possibly every way to build a business. I had no idea. I stayed up until midnight thinking about it, so I only got 2 and a half hours of sleep that night. My goal the next morning was to beat Clay to the office and prove to him how dedicated I was. I got to the office at 3:30 a.m. and my plan was to be waiting in his office when he arrived. I pull into the parking lot and I see his van already there. I walked in and he was building a website for one of his clients. Yes, he has a team that builds websites, but he wanted to design the website for this client personally. I walk in with my moleskine notebook that I take notes in along with my pen, highlighter, and a book Clay wrote called BOOM. I brought my moleskine notebook because Clay told me shortly after I got hired, "You're human and you are inevitably going to forget stuff. Go buy a notebook to write down anything you learn. Your brain is for thinking, your pen is for remembering."

I saw that the one he was carrying was a moleskine one so obviously I went and tried to buy the exact same kind. I sat down and Clay said, "What's up man?" I replied, " Not much". That was all that was said for the next hour as he continued editing the website page. Once he stopped editing, he then pulled out his clipboard with his to do list that he has on him 24/7. He uses Google Sheets to make and edit it. He starts deleting things on the computer that he had previously marked off the day before and adding things that he wrote down in pen on his to-do list.

He pulled up his calendar and showed me that from 5 a.m. to 6 a.m. he has meta time which means "self and time for self" (for those wondering this was before the Metaverse.) He said, "Every single successful person I have ever met or have interviewed on my podcast has had a to do list and a calendar. They intentionally plan out each hour, day, and moment of their lives. Every single morning you have to update your to do list from the previous day and print off your to-do list and calendar. You absolutely can not have it on your phone. There are too many distractions that pop up. If you do this, you spend your day being reactive instead of being proactive."

I feel you wanting to argue about it being on your phone and not printing it off. Every one of Clay's business coaching clients argue about this with him. They always want to use an app or something on their phone or tablet. Here are some facts about that.

Time Flies: U.S. Adults Now Spend Nearly Half a Day Interacting with Media

https://www.nielsen.com/us/en/insights/article/2018/time-flies-us-adults-now-spend-nearly-half-a-day-interacting-with-media/

Research published by the University of Chicago found that even if cell phones are turned off, turned face down or put away their mere presence reduces people's cognitive capacity."

https://www.cnbc.com/2019/01/18/research-shows-that-cell-phones-distract-students--so-france-banned-them-in-school--. html#targetText=Research%20published%20by%20the%20 University,presence%20reduces%20people's%20cognitive%20capacity.

Fact - New Study Shows You're Wasting 21.8 hours a Week - The business leaders we polled spent 6.8 hours per week on low value business activities that they could easily have paid somebody else $50/hour or less to handle for them. They wasted 3.9 hours each week indulging in what we might call escapist "mental health breaks" --streaming YouTube videos and checking social media. They wasted 3.4 hours a week handling low-value emails and 3.2 hours a week dealing with low-value interruptions that easily could have been handled by somebody else on staff. They spent 1.8 hours a week handling low-value requests from co-workers and another 1.8 hours a week putting out preventable fires. Finally, they spent an average of 1 hour each week sitting in completely non-productive or wasteful meetings. Total that up and we're looking at 21.8 wasted hours each week -- hours that are going up in smoke while you're doing things that contribute little to no value to your company.

https://www.inc.com/david-finkel/new-study-shows-youre-wasting-218-hours-a-week.html

You might be upset right now because what Clay showed me wasn't a get rich quick scheme, investment strategies or some motivational speech. One thing this book is NOT is a shortcut to riches. This is not a motivational book.

However, you might find some motivation from it. But motivation isn't what makes drastic changes in your life. Motivation and inspiration play their part. I love getting motivation from people like David Goggins, Jocko Willink, Clay Clark, and Cameron Haynes. People who most of the world calls insane. I look at them and get motivated. It's nice seeing them and realizing it's okay to have a magnificent obsession with something and to never be satisfied, especially where the rest of the world would tell me that's not OK.

If you're never satisfied, you need to go see a counselor and talk about a safe place and "realistic" goals. That's complete bull. Motivation fades, the discipline to schedule things and stay on track every single day is what truly changes your life. There are going to be days when that alarm clock goes off and your inner voice is coming up with all the excuses on why you need to hit snooze. Clay Clark talks about it all the time, but he hasn't had, a sick day in 23 years. He says when people are sick, feel bad or have personal problems they hit pause on their business and life. This just causes more personal problems and issues and then you're stuck in the doom loop.

That inner voice is powerful, but you still need to block out time to actually get stuff done. If you don't schedule time to work on proactive things in your calendar you will only do things when you're motivated to do them and you will inevitably fail. If you don't become a disciple of discipline, that inner voice is going to tear you apart. It's the voice that's there in the morning at 3:30 a.m. telling you to crawl back in your warm bed. It's the voice telling you that your legs hurt and you shouldn't go on that run. It's the voice telling you that you need to sleep and the deadline is a suggestion. It's the voice telling you "maybe other people are right and I should give up". It's the voice that says, "I'll do it tomorrow."

"Will you sleep, or what deadlines will you keep?"

Clay Clark

(Founder of Thrive15.com and former U.S. Small Business Administration Entrepreneur of the Year)

META TIME

What is meta time and how do you do it? You need to have half an hour to an hour blocked off in your schedule every day to do design your days and your life. This is where you plan your day and go over your to do list, and calendar. Meta time is non-negotiable if you want to be successful and reach whatever your goals are. Clay says, "Every single super successful person I have interviewed has time blocked off to plan their day and a to-do list."

For me, meta time was an absolute game changer even though it is so simple and boring. I used to be like a dog

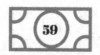

with zoomies: I have no idea where I'm going but I'm going to get there fast and with maximum effort. I've always had a great work ethic and drive, but I've also let being reactive control my life and used it as a crutch on why I couldn't get things done. I would focus on 18 things at once and end up getting some of things somewhat done and the rest sorta, kinda, not really done at all. In college, what would happen every single day is, I would sit down to study, read two lines, and remember I was supposed to move over the laundry before one of the other roommates got back home.

I'd get up to move the laundry over and on the way to do that I saw my tower of beer cans that I and others worked so hard to build last night had fallen over. Obviously, I stopped to fix it, then I decided I should actually throw these away and threw them out. I sat back down to do homework and out of habit, opened YouTube, saw the trailer for the new Lion King movie came out. I got excited, watched it, then felt hungry so I made food, which was two packs of Ramen noodles, two cans of tuna, relish, and honey.

I sat down to eat, but if I'm eating I need to be watching something, so I turned on the original Lion King movie. Then, my alarm went off, meaning it was time to stop doing homework and it was time to go get shots up before my basketball practice. Then after practice I came back to roommates upset that my laundry wasn't moved over and I was upset because I still had homework to do. That's a true story by the way. Instances like this were an everyday thing. I never had any idea of what I needed to get done, and even if I did, I never scheduled it to actually get done. The only things I had scheduled were things that other people would put on my schedule, like, my practices, classes, class schedule, or team meetings. None of my things were actually scheduled by me. I was highly motivated to work out, train, and be the best player in that league, so I was always in the weight room or in the gym training, but I never knew what I was going to do until I got there. When I got to the gym, I would waste 15 minutes debating with myself on what I was going to do. Same thing when I went to the weight room. I had no idea what I was going to do until I got there.

I was motivated and dedicated, but without an actual plan or accountability. These habits didn't start or end at college; they stayed with me until I met Clay. It seems so simple to make a to-do list and calendar, but that alone changed my life. I currently accomplish in one day what it would've taken me a week to accomplish. That's in no way an exaggeration.

I have a question for you: What do Clay Clark, David Goggins, my college self, myself now, Robert Kiosaki, you, and the homeless person in your city have in common? We all have 24 hours in a day. We all have the same amount of time, yet people will complain that they don't

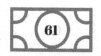

have enough time to do anything. That's simply not true. How we choose to spend it matters. According to Forbes, "Americans spent, on average, 1,300 hours on social media last year." That's around three and a half hours a day on social media. People are constantly responding to social media notifications, text messages, or Facetimes. You have to block out time in your calendar to actually get stuff done. Most people spend their day being reactive instead of proactive. When you have stuff scheduled in your calendar you must not stray from the path you set for yourself. What gets scheduled gets done. You have to be able to self-motivate and stay disciplined without the help of anyone else. Now, let's into the process of the to-do list and calendar.

> "The secret of your success is
> determined by your daily agenda."

 John Maxwell

John Calvin Maxwell is an American author, speaker, and pastor who has written many books, primarily focusing on leadership. Titles include The 21 Irrefutable Laws of Leadership and The 21 Indispensable Qualities of a Leader.

CALENDAR

You must turn your calendar into your accountability partner. When Clay talks about the calendar he says there are rocks and sand. Rocks are immovable blocks of time that you have committed to do something intentional. This would be like Clay's meeting with clients or interviews on shows. They cannot move and they must be there. Sand refers to to-do items that have to get done. However, they can be done in between rocks. Now let me give you a heads up on where people fall short. Most people I've seen use "sand" for time to go on social media and respond to Snap chats or the mean comment somebody left on Facebook. Don't. Use "sand" to be productive and knock out action items. Action items are just things on your to do list that don't merit an actual spot on the calendar. Clay cannot be reached 90% of the time. It is not because Clay is mean, but it's because he is intentionally proactive and not reactive.

People can not just add stuff to his calendar. People will ask for meetings all the time, lunches and dinners. Clay will not do it. You might be thinking, "JT that's great, but I want to have a movie night with my wife, or go golfing on Sundays." That is awesome. That's why you figure out your F6 goals and then you schedule it into your calendar. Currently Clay has family time scheduled Wednesdays 6:30-11 p.m. and Fridays 5:30-9:30 p.m., then Sundays are dedicated to church and family. Now you might be saying "Woah, woah that's not enough" or "I only want to schedule date night with my wife once a week."

Whatever your personal goals are, that's what you need to schedule. Clay's goals aren't my goals or your goals, and that's the point. The point of this book is to help you get to where you want to be, not where I want you to be. We use Google Calendar, you can use whatever you want, but make sure you actually use it and schedule everything. Use whatever color scheme you want, just don't make it super complicated. Your goal is to never show up late to anything ever. There are some people that have no idea how time

Official Clay Clark Calendar		Mon Sep 11, 2023 (Central Time - Chicago)
6am	6:00 - Nathan - Complete Carpet - CC 6am - 7am	
7am	Clay meets with the coaches 7am - 8am	
8am	Elephant in the Room Management Meeting 8am - 9am	
9am	Clay meets with all team members 9am - 10am	
10am	Clay meets with Kenny & Highway Man Signs 10am - 11am	
11am	Clay Calls Papagalios - ████ Tricia & Dave - CC 11am - 12pm	11:15 AM - Clay meets with Jared & Jennifer ████ 11:30am - 12pm
12pm	Clay is interviewed by Pamela ████ - CC 12pm - 1pm	
1pm	Clay meets with Thomas ████ CC 1pm - 1:30pm	
	Clay meets with Josh ████ 1:30pm - 2pm	
2pm	Clay interviews Peter ████ 2pm - 2:30pm	
	Clay is interviewed by Mel K - CC 2:30pm - 3:30pm	
3pm		
	Clay and Z Record Podcast - CC 3:30pm - 5pm	3:00 PM - Clay interviews Dr. Mark ████ CC - CC 3:30pm - 4pm
4pm		Clay interviews Matt ████ 4pm - 4:30pm
		Clay is interviewed on the kennel with VINNDOGG radio - ████
5pm	Clay is interviewed on freedom talk CounterCulture - ████ 5pm - 5:30pm	
	Clay is interviewed on the Big Mig ████ 5:30pm - 6pm	
6pm	Clay Clark Works On Big Project - CC 6pm - 7pm	13 Point Assessment / Interview - CC 6pm - 6:30pm
		13 Point Assessment / Interview - CC 6:30pm - 7pm
7pm	13 Point Assessment / Interview - CC 7pm - 7:30pm	
	13 Point Assessment / Interview - CC 7:30pm - 8pm	

works and are late to absolutely everything. That is not "cool" and that is no longer you. If you schedule meetings, dinner, class schedule, a doggy play date, it doesn't matter, just schedule it on your calendar and get there on time. Here is a picture of Clay's calendar:

"Don't turn your failure to plan into an emergency for others."

Clay Clark

(Founder of Thrive15.com and former U.S. Small Business Administration Entrepreneur of the Year)

TO DO LIST

Your to-do list is nothing complicated. Don't make it unnecessarily complicated. We use spreadsheet. Column A and B, and that's it. In column B, you write in what the action item is. In column A, you can label it if you want to, but everything on there needs to get done anyway, so don't make it complicated. I only label it if I need to connect with someone to get it done. So if I have something on my to-do list like, 'Call Clay about speaker wanting to be a guest on the ThriveTime Show,' then in column A I'll label it "Clay". That's as complicated as I make it. You want to print your to-do list out daily. No, you cannot use notes on your phone, or use Google Sheets on your phone. I don't care what app you have. I don't care if you also put your phone on Do Not Disturb. Distractions are too easily

accessible when they're on your phone. Stop trying to debate me in your head and just print it off every morning. If you don't have a clipboard, printer or computer, go mow someone's lawn, have a car wash party in a Speedo, or set up a lemonade stand. I don't care how you get the money. You either make excuses or you find solutions. Since you printed your to-do list off, you will highlight anything that you get done. Clay uses a red Expo marker. Use whatever you want, just make sure you can still see the words after you highlight them.

If you have a new thought pop into your head throughout that day, write it somewhere on the to-do list. You no longer have the mindset of, "Oh, I'll remember to do that." Assume you're going to forget it in the next ten seconds. I know you, the reader, would never do this (insert sarcasm). Do not use other people as a to-do list. Stop saying, "Will you remind me to..." They will not remember. It would be like writing your to do list on an Etch-a-Sketch and having it in your pocket when you go play bumper cars. Don't allow other people to do it to you either. Unless they are your boss, they don't have the privilege to just add stuff to your to do list. The brain is for thinking, the pen is for remembering. So if you drive by a dry cleaners and think, "I need to take that suit to get dry cleaned," write it down! The next morning during meta time you will have a spreadsheet pulled up on the computer, and yesterday's to-do list in front of you.

1	Call EOFire.com - Approve interview time
2	Upload - HIS GLORY'S "HOLY LAND" VIDEO FILE - RE: Simulcast this weekend of His Glory's movie, Holy Land (see document)
3	Upload Liz Show -
4	Watch Amanda Grace Episode - https://www.youtube.com/live/AsSMv0ynHOM?si=KO-jxq3a3dRg500Y
5	Create Mass Text Message
6	BH-PM.com - Create Mass Text Message
7	Call Andrew - Update ZIP Recruiter
8	Call Andrew - Purple Rain - 1. Secure office space 2. Add the address to the website 3. Secure Google Map 4. Get 40 Google Reviews
9	Andrew - Now Hiring - Are candidates being called?
10	Andrew - Review Calls - Are review calls being made?
11	Bunkie - Is mall Kiosk.staffing arranged?
12	Call Haleigh - Followup on letter of recommendation / Glass door
13	Call Devin - Change the Liz thumbnail
14	Call Andrew - Add epic images to the google maps at ThriveTime show
15	Call Devin - Log into Facebook
16	Call Kash Patel (Get Trump & Bongino to Florida)
17	Call Andrew - Pro Day Sports - Get reviews
18	Call Devin - Download the New Mexico Governor Video Again
19	Call Andrew - Focus On Junk In The Trunk after launching Purple Rain - https://docs.google.com/document/d/13zaWxL6_O__1NbObPPnOfZJG6BHV7O1f8LNIkzuqeSs/edit?usp=sharing

Anything you crossed off, delete it off of your spreadheet. Anything you wrote down, add it onto Sheets. Now print it off. Lather, rinse, repeat. Here is a picture of Clay's to do list.

MORE PRO-TIPS FROM CLAY
FOR TIME MANAGEMENT

» Every day wake up before anyone else in your house does

» Commit to getting everything on your list done every day

» Only work via appointment

» Only engage in mutually beneficial relationships

» Only focus on what you can control

» Pay experts and charge if you are one

What do Clay Clark, David Goggins, my parents, Steve Jobs, and the person living in the van down by the river all have in common? They all have 24 hours in the day. You have heard this before and it isn't a complicated statement, yet it's a profound statement. However, I must mention it again because it just doesn't click for most people. Since being a business coach and being around business owners, the number one excuse people give me for not being able to get stuff done is, "I don't have enough time." Every single time, they will use the excuse of time. Here are a couple I have heard recently:

"It was the holidays, I had people over and didn't have enough time to write content for my website. "

"I know I should be doing meta time but I don't have time to do it."

"I have kids so it's impossible to schedule stuff. They have practice and other things and it changes."

"I can't get to the gym to workout anymore because I am in the building phase of my business."

Now I know you reading this book would never use these excuses. I know you take full accountability for your actions. There are 24 hours in the day for everyone. Unless it's 2040 and Elon Musk has now successfully populated Mars, then you'd have an extra 37 minutes per day.

"The average American spends 5 hours per day watching TV."

https://www.nytimes.com/2016/07/01/business/media/nielsen-survey-media-viewing.html

"The average American devotes nearly 10 hours per day to screen time."

http://www.cnn.com/2016/06/30/health/americans-screen-time-nielsen/index.html

Imagine if you got that time back. Let's be real with each other for a second. You know right now what you're spending too much time on. Maybe it's video games, TV, social media, watching YouTube videos of monkeys throwing poop on visitors, or fantasy football. I don't have any video games in my house. Not because I don't like them, but because I know I'll like them too much. There are literally people who play Grand Theft Auto, spending hours and hours, using real money to buy a Ferrari or lamborghini IN THE GAME, then go to "car meet ups" IN THE GAME, only to impress their friends IN THE GAME.

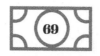

Here is a profound idea: instead of trying to live your dream life through video games, go make it happen in real life. There is a video game about farming where you literally plow fields and take care of livestock, grow corn, etc., to make money. They play it for hours and hours everyday. Why would you not just go get a job on a farm? None of this makes sense to me, but people do it. Then they turn around and make excuses about not having time to do the things that will actually benefit them. We live in a world where it's getting easier and easier to get massive dopamine hits while needing to expend less and less effort to receive it. Whether it's video games, porn, Tik Toks, or YouTube Shorts. We are hardwired to do things instantly and not delay gratification. People often say to me, "It sounds like you don't have any self control if you can't allow yourself to have any video game console any more," or, "If you delete the social media apps it's because you don't have self control. Shouldn't you just work on self control?"

The answer is absolutely not. I know how humans work. I know we are hardwired to take gratification instantly. I'm not going to try to fight biology or human nature. It's like a chess game, I'm not going to try to change the rules. Instead, I'm going to find the most strategic way to win within the rules. So, I'm going to cut out those distractions. I don't have a TV in my living room or bedroom because I know if it's there, I'll watch it. My phone is absolutely never allowed in my bed. That way, my body knows that when I get in bed it's time to sleep. How many times have you heard someone say they have trouble sleeping, but they go to sleep with the TV on or with their phone scrolling social media?

They say, "I need it to fall asleep," or they say, " I've tried sleeping without it before and it doesn't work. I still can't fall asleep." OBVIOUSLY! It's because you tried it for one night and your body isn't used to it. It's like the person who says, "I've tried diets and going to the gym. It's just my genetics that don't work." No, it's because you're filled with jackassary and you tried it for one week then gave up because you didn't see results. If you get to the gym 5 days a week, every week for a year, you will have no choice but to lose weight and build muscle. I don't care what you do at the gym. Go to the gym every day, eat a donut, and leave. Do it just to prove me wrong. Eventually you're going to be around fit people all the time and you're going to think "I'm here already, I might as well do something".

When it comes to making time for things and if you truly want to be successful, you will find time to do the things you need to do. You know the things that are a waste of time and you need to cut out. You're waiting for a secret way to not want to do those things or to not have the desire to do those things. It'll help you out if it doesn't exist. You're always going to want to do that. Now that I own a dog training business, I'll use dog training as an example. When presented with a choice, a dog will choose the higher value object every time. For example, say you have a bag of treats. That treat to the dog is worth, in our terms, about $10. This is outstanding unless you go outside and the dog sees a squirrel. To the dog, that squirrel is worth $5,000, and that treat no longer means anything. So when you say, 'Come,' the dog thinks, "Who cares? I'm taking the higher value" and chases the squirrel. There are different types of dog training. Treat training is considered positive reinforcement. Negative reinforcement would be like a shock collar. Basically, if the dog doesn't do what you ask, you light it up on the shock collar. Now, let's say you teach the dog, 'Come.' If the dog comes, it gets a treat. If the dog doesn't, it gets lit up on the shock collar. Now the dog has a fear attached to not coming (FYI this is NOT how we train at MakeYourDogEpic.com. If you're interested in how we train check out the website; we use focus-based positive reinforcement training and the Make Your Dog Epic method. That was an absolutely shameless plug for my business.) After using the shock collar, if you take the dog outside and it chases after the squirrel, and you say 'Come,' the dog now listens. Not because you're saying 'Come' is worth more to the dog, but because it now fears getting lit up on the shock collar. The dog still has the thoughts, "I need to chase this squirrel and murder it." The thoughts don't disappear or go away. The dog now just has a fear attached to not coming when called.

I fear not being successful. I fear living my whole life and not doing any of the stuff that I was meant to do. I fear dying and not one person remembering who I was. One of the people who has impacted my mindset is David Goggins. He sums up my fears very well. David Goggins isn't religious, but he said this during an interview with Joe Rogan, and I have the same view on life. I'll paraphrase, but he basically says that he imagines he is in this big long line to get into Heaven. Then he gets to God and God shows him a chart with his name on it. At the top it says his name,, and then lists out many accomplishments under it: Navy Seal, Army Ranger, world record for most pull ups in 24 hours, ran multiple 100 miles races, and 250 mile races. Then David says to God, "The name is right, but I haven't done any of that stuff." God replies, "I know. But you were supposed to." That gives me goosebumps every time I hear it. If you want to hear his full quote, go to YouTube and type in "David Goggins biggest fear." It should be the first one that pops up with Joe Rogan.

If I have my computer and Xbox in front of me where I can write this book or play video games, I'm going to WANT to play video games. But I FEAR not being successful, so I'll write the book. However, I can just take the distraction away and just not have an Xbox. It's like having a trained dog, but never needing to see a squirrel. They put on blinders on horses even though they are trained. Why try to go against nature when you can just take the distractions out of your life and get your time back? Time is the most valuable resource. Don't waste it doing unproductive things.

» When are you going to start using a calendar?

» When are you going to schedule meta time?

» What are you currently doing in your life that you will cut out now?

CHAPTER 4
MENTORS

"The A team is rarely available, the
B team is readily available"

Clay Clark

(Founder of Thrive15.com and former U.S. Small Business
Administration Entrepreneur of the Year)

"You are the average of the five people
you spend the most time with"

Jim Rohn

(Emanuel James Rohn, professionally known as Jim Rohn, was
an American entrepreneur, author and motivational speaker.)

"He that walketh with wise men
shall be wise: but a companion
of fools shall be destroyed."

John 13:20

THIS IS HOW I MET CLAY CLARK.

I had planned on going back to college in Canada for one more year to play basketball. It literally would've just been to play basketball. I would've taken 1 class a semester just to be eligible and I didn't even need the credits to graduate. Then Covid happened, so I started delivering for Amazon because it was one of the only jobs I could find. Plus, I needed to earn money and to save money to be able to go back to school. Then I found out my school wasn't going to have a basketball season, so I decided to find a gym I could get training at as well as shadow the owner at so I could learn how to manage a gym. At that point, my goal was to open my own gym and train kids to play basketball once my basketball career was over. So, I messaged a gym on Facebook that I used to train at and asked if I could work for free. They asked me to come in, and ended up offering me a job. I took it and used the gym to work and train.

My schedule consisted of working for Amazon, the gym, and training for basketball when I wasn't working. That went on for a couple months. At the gym, we had a team meeting on Mondays at 3 p.m. where we talked about weekly wins, what we could do better, and also went through this book called, 'Dragon Energy - the Mindset Kanye, Trump, and You Need To Succeed,' that was written by Clay Clark. I learned that Clay Clark was actually located in Jenks, Oklahoma, and was the gym's business coach. He did their website, marketing, advertising, sales, systems, workflow design, proforma creation, business model design, etc. I had just left college with a Business Administration degree. Well, almost. I still have to write one more paper to get my degree (Don't tell my mom. She thinks I graduated, but didn't have a ceremony because of Covid. I didn't lie to her, I just haven't corrected her). I was thinking I should know everything that Clay talks about because I would've learned it in college from my business professors. Then I realized, not once did one of my professors talk about mindset, systems, making a call script, the Dream 100, search engine optimization, online advertising, or almost anything he talked about. I was super intrigued by this book and who Clay Clark was.

The trainer talked about him like he was a mythical being who didn't sleep and was all-knowing when it came to business. I had been working for this gym for a couple months at this point and the trainer asked if I wanted to go with him to Clay's business coaching meeting Friday mornings. I immediately responded, "Hell yes." I met him at Clay's office Friday morning and I was expecting a very corporate looking office with bright light. Where everything looks very modern and shiny. I walked in and immediately thought I was at a dive bar. Edison bulbs everywhere, posters hanging from the ceiling, old barn wood with picture frames all over the walls, and a Ford Model T right when you walk in. Then, I see Clay in AND1 shorts, Yeezys and a hoodie.

He was on the phone talking while simultaneously marking things off his to-do list. Everything was the exact opposite of what I was expecting for a meeting with someone who built 13 multimillion dollar businesses. We

met and told him I had just graduated with a Business Administration degree from a college in Canada. He immediately started calling me 'Captain Canada' and speaking in a Canadian accent. I loved it. It was a great way to start the meeting on a high note and break the ice. In the meeting they went over the action items Clay's team got done and also the action items the other trainer did, or didn't get done.

Clay went over multiple other things and assigned more homework. After that meeting, I was hooked and knew I had to learn from different perspectives to be more successful. I remembered my uncle talking about a book called 'Rich Dad, Poor Dad,' and how it was a completely different view of how most people think about money. I figured if I didn't have any mentors currently in my life to help, I'll get mentors from books, even though I hate reading with a passion. I went to Barnes and Noble and bought a copy of *Rich Dad Poor Dad*. I read that whole book in a couple days. I bought a highlighter and planned on highlighting everything I had never heard before. I was basically highlighting every word on every page. No one had ever told me anything like this. I remember while reading it the whole time I was thinking, "Why doesn't everyone do this? Everyone needs to read this book."

After I read the book, I went back to Barnes and Noble and bought Robert Kiyosaki's second book, 'Cashflow Quadrant,' as well as 5 more copies of 'Rich Dad Poor Dad.' I had to get these books to my friends and family. I gave 4 out to friends and 1 to my parents and begged them to read it. I was so excited for them. If we all read it and got on the same page (no pun intended) we could all be financially successful and not have to live paycheck to paycheck in the rat race. I gave out 5 books. Guess how many people read the book?

Not one person I bought the book for has read it. I stopped checking in after a couple months. It was so frustrating that all the answers could be in front of you, but you don't want to take the time to open the book and learn. I even bought my sister the teen version of 'Rich Dad Poor Dad.' She was 21 at the time, but I knew she wouldn't read the full version. Yes, as you guessed, she hasn't read it. That was over a year ago. Recently, she told me she never wanted financial advice from me and then at the same dinner asked me to buy her the most expensive thing on

her wedding registry. Complete jackassary. People who I bought the book for still complain about money issues but won't read the book. In Robert Kiyosaki's book *Cash Flow Quadrant*, talks about how there are 4 main ways to make money: Employee, Self Employed, Business, and Investor. Robert Kiyosaki says be careful who you take advice from. You don't want to get all your advice from employees or the self-employed. I realized every single person in my life was in the employee quadrant. It helped open my eyes and I knew I had to find a mentor not just from books but someone in person. Clay Clark was the only person I knew that owned businesses.

The gym's heater went out one weekend and instead of finding solutions, the owner closed the gym. I loved it because it was the same weekend Clay had one of his business conferences. I asked the trainer if we would be able to go and he said he would text Clay. Clay responded, "Absolutely." The trainer made some excuses as to why he couldn't go. Keep in mind, it was at the time we would've been working anyways, but somehow he couldn't make it.

During the conference, my mind was getting blown left and right. You don't know what you don't know. I'm sitting there with my mind blown (also slightly pissed) because I didn't learn any of this in college. Then Clay Staires, not to be confused with Clay Clark, gets up and talks about his journey and have his journey started after he read 'Rich

Dad Poor Dad.' He was in his 50's when he made a change in his life. Shortly after had a break in the conference.

I went up to Clay Staires and told him about how I read two of Robert Kiyosaki's books and how I bought one for my parents, but they still hadn't read it. Even though they are in the same situation he was in a couple years ago. It was uncanny, the similarities between them. Both my parents were teachers. Clay Staires was also a teacher. Clay Staires was in his 50's when he decided to make a change. My parents were currently in their 50's. I just knew he could help, but he let me down easy and said, "You can't want something for someone else. All you can do is what you did."

I asked him how to get mentors in my life and he told me I should go ask Clay Clark that question. The break ends and in my head I'm trying to plan out how I'm going to ask Clay and when would be a good time. I decided I'm going to do it during lunch. I kept rehearsing in my mind what I was going to say. It was like I was in middle school again, planning to ask a girl out for the first time. (Side note: in middle school, she said yes, then brought 12 friends with her and they all sat right behind us at the movie theater. Talk about nerves and awkwardness). Then, they break for lunch and Clay goes straight into his "Box that Rocks," which is his podcast room/office where he does client meetings. He went in there right at 12 and went straight into a client meeting. This rocked my world again because even though he was putting on a conference, he was still making meetings happen.

I waited until the next break. I went up to him and he said, "I'm happy you're here." I told him about how I read the book and the different quadrants and asked how I could get mentors in my life that are on the right side of the quadrant. He replied, "Come work for me." I responded, "Deal!" I didn't care if I was going to be working for free or just following him around and getting him coffee. It did not matter, I just needed to learn. He asked what hours I worked for the basketball gym, and we worked out a schedule so that I could do both. At that point it began. I worked for Clay from 6 a.m. to 3 p.m. and worked at the gym from 4 p.m. to 9 p.m. Rinse and repeat. For a little bit, I still delivered for Amazon on Sundays, but soon after I quit my job at Amazon, that way I could work for Clay on Sundays.

I wanted to tell some of that story because it's important to understand both times I propelled myself into better positions. I wasn't worried about the paychecks or the health care or benefits. I just needed to learn. Robert Kiyosaki and Clay Clark both talk about this process: Work to LEARN, Work to EARN, and Work to RETURN (teach others). Both my parents are teachers and each time I told them I got a new job and learning experience, their next two questions were, "How much do you get paid and do you get benefits?" This is absolutely the wrong mindset. As I'm writing this, I can feel you arguing with me in your head. Most people don't understand this at first and always push back. The moment you start working for money you stop trying to learn and figure out how to make your money work for you. I was so excited to tell my parents. "Guys I just got offered a job by a guy who is the U.S. SBA Entrepreneur of the Year for the State of Oklahoma, the founder of several multi-million dollar companies, has had the number 1 business podcast on iTunes 6x! He talks about the same stuff Robert Kiyosaki talks about." Immediately my dad said, "Well, with that many businesses he better be paying you a lot." I responded, "We didn't talk about that. I'm probably going to be working for free." They couldn't wrap their heads around the point of that.

Clay Clark's Man Cave

You 100% need a mentor. As I pointed out earlier you can get them through books or people. I recommend both and so does Clay. You might be saying to yourself, "Well Clay doesn't have mentors." This is a picture of his man cave. All of the books you see have been read, highlighted through, and notes taken in. No, he didn't buy these books just for looks. You can pick up any of the books and they are highlighted through and marked up. All of these books have been read and serve as mentors for Clay. Now, a lot of people think they have everything figured out. Robert H. Zoellner says the first step is admitting that you need a mentor. Clay said if he has ever felt stuck he has paid for mentors.

Either it was paying to spend the whole day with the founder of Hobby Lobby or spend a couple hours with the founder of QuikTrip. He would also pay for books or for seminars. Most people think they have everything figured out. However, you picked up this book, so I believe you know you need a mentor. Maybe you're at a point in your life where you are already "successful". That's phenomenal. However, you don't know what you don't know. It could also be time for you to start mentoring someone else. Then maybe you'll get to the point where you have multiple businesses or are very successful.

So, maybe you are at a point where you not only need to be looking up for mentors, but also looking down to see who you can mentor.

When looking for a mentor, be aware of a couple things. First thing is, the B team is readily available to be your mentor. The A team is not readily available. The people at the top of their industry are going to be very hard to get a hold of. The top leaders or successful people are hard to reach. That's because people like Clay, Dr. Robert Zollener, Michael Levine, John Stockton, and others have built a wall around them either physically or digitally. For instance, Clay never leaves the office to do lunches or networking because he has literally built the environment he wants to be in. His office looks like a dive bar mixed with a tropical resort. It has a massive fire pit, a waterfall that you can walk under, goats, chickens, even bunnies. There is music playing that he likes. At this point in his life, he has surrounded himself with employees and partners that he likes. The B team is readily available. You can find them at any coffee shop, ready to pitch their pyramid scheme and mentor others. They are ready to teach you all their SUPER moves and BEST practices even though they have never done it.

**HERE ARE A COUPLE OPTIONS
ON HOW TO GET A MENTOR THAT
CLAY CLARK AND HIS MENTOR
DR. ZOELLNER SUGGEST**

» Option 1 - Pay them

» Option 2 - Intern

» Option 3 - Do work for free

» Option 4 - Find someone
who is close to them.

» Option 5 - Attended the workshops
or conferences that they attended

» Option 6 - Relentlessly cold call
them and try to pick their brain

» Option 7 - Schedule them
for an interview

Option 1 is you pay them. That's right, you pay them to learn. People are willing to pay hundreds of thousands of dollars to go to college to learn from people who have never actually done what they teach. A much more effective move, is to pay someone who has actually done it. For example, Michael Levine is the PR consultant for NIKE, Prince, Michael Jackson, and others. Clay asked Michael Levine to pick his brain. He said no. Clay offered to pay him, he said no. Clay asked how much it would cost to make it happen. Clay had to pay him $20,000 for 5 hours of his time. At the time this book is being edited, (August 2023), Clay recently paid a man $10,000 for just one hour of his time.

Option 2 is to intern. This is a great move to learn from a mentor. If you're at a point in your life where you aren't sure what you want to do. Look around at businesses in industries you would possibly like to work in. Make a list of the top businesses and email, call, and visit them to offer to intern for free. Best-case, you get to be around someone you want mentoring you or you decide that the specific industry is perfect and you'd love to work in it. My personal thoughts are that before anyone goes to college they should intern for a minimum of 6 months in the industry they want to go to school for. No one says no to someone wanting to intern for free. If they say they don't have a spot for you, tell them you'll clean the bathrooms for free just to be there, and mean it. Maybe 3 months in you realize you hate it. Now you can just stop interning after 3 months instead of spending years in school and thousands and thousands of dollars to find out that you hate it.

Option 3 is to do work for free. This is different from interning for free. If you are able to provide some sort of service for someone, offer to work for free. If you can mow yards, clean pools, clean bathrooms, etc..., offer to do it for free. If you go into a business your mentor operates and you offer to clean bathrooms for free for a week or a month

in order to meet with them for an hour, that's a move. Clay has done work for QuikTrip, a professional sports team, Outback Steakhouse, and for multiple other places, all for free at a time when he did not have time or money to spare to do it. He made it happen anyways.

Option 4 is to find someone who is close to them. Maybe they aren't reachable, but someone close to them is. Reach them and try to work it out. For example, Clay went to lunch with his now mentor, Robert Zoellner, because he asked relentlessly and his wife worked for Dr. Zoellner.

Option 5 is to attend workshops or conferences that they attended. As I said, that's how I got Clay to be my mentor. I went to one of his conferences and actually asked, "How do I get mentors that are business owners in my life?" He responded, "come work for me." With no hesitation, I said, "Deal" . We didn't talk about pay, hours, or anything. I would've done it for free. If it would have been for free it still would've been the best decision I've ever made. I learned more from Clay Clark in 1 week of working for him than I did in 5 years of college and $45,000 in tuition.. That is not an exaggeration.

Option 6 is to relentlessly cold call them. For example, Clay has been trying to get John Stockton on his show for over 5 years and he kept telling him no. John Stockton is arguably the greatest point guard to ever play the game of basketball. Clay has been asking to interview him on his show for years. After years of emails and calls, Stockton finally said yes. You can either learn from years of failures and struggles or you can have a mentor.

As a note, option 7 is to reach out to mentors and to interview them on your podcast or to be a featured content contributor for a book you are writing.

Clay Clark has mentored through the years is Clay Staires. I recently read Clay Staires book Grow - The Field Guide To Personal Growth. This is an excerpt from his book.

"Do you have a counselor, a coach, or a book? What is the source of your new revelation going to be? There must be a reliable source which cannot just be you! This part of the process of learning how to learn. If you learn it all by yourself, you would never learn empathy and compassion for others. You would be self-sufficient and have no need for anyone else. That is the wrong path or, as Yoda might say, "the path to the dark side this is."

» Luke Skywalker had Yoda

» Neo had Morpheus

» Alejandro had Zorro

» The Karate Kid had Mr. Miyagi

> » Even Kung Fu Panda had the little white fuzzy animal (I never was quite sure what that thing was!).

> » But the real question is, "Who do you have?" Who will be your Yoda?"

There aren't many beneficial hacks in life but having mentors is one of them. You don't know what you don't know. Don't try to come up with new ideas or reinvent the wheel. Use mentors to give you a hand up.

"People don't need a handout, they need a hand up".

Clay Clark
(Founder of Thrive15.com and former U.S. Small Business Administration Entrepreneur of the Year)

"To avoid criticism, say nothing, do nothing, be nothing."

Aristotle
(Aristotle was an Ancient Greek philosopher and polymath. His writings cover a broad range of subjects spanning the natural sciences, philosophy, linguistics, economics, politics, psychology and the arts)

POST CHAPTER REVIEW

» Who could be your mentor?

» What are you willing to sacrifice to learn from a mentor?

» What authors could you read as your mentors?

» Where will you find your mentors?

CHAPTER 5

IT'S 100% YOUR FAULT,YOUR SUCCESS IS 100% UP TO YOU

"Extreme ownership. Leaders must own everything in their world. There is no one else to blame."

Jocko Willink

(John Gretton "Jocko" Willink Jr. is an American author, podcaster, and retired United States Navy officer who served in the Navy SEALs and is a former member of SEAL Team 3, and best-selling author of *Extreme Ownership*.)

"If you're remarkable, it's likely that some people won't like you. That's part of the definition of remarkable. Nobody gets unanimous praise–ever. The best the timid can hope for is to be unnoticed. Criticism comes to those who stand out."

Seth Godin

(Bestselling author, entrepreneur and marketing expert.)

If I haven't offended you yet, here it comes. In a free country,where you are in life is exactly where you deserve to be. Read that line again and again until it registers and you stop thinking of reasons why it wouldn't be true. If you don't have the job you want, it's your fault. If your business isn't growing it's your fault. You might be thinking,"But

JT, people just aren't spending as much money currently." No, they just aren't spending it on your product and it's your fault. If you're overweight, it's your fault. Now, some of you are going to bring up genetics or you're going to bring up people who have some sort of chronic condition. Stop using 1% of cases for your excuse to be a couch potato. If you enjoy having a victim mentality and enjoy blaming others you aren't going to enjoy this chapter. One of the most beneficial things I've learned from book mentors and Clay is that I have to own everything in my life. I know you want to argue with me, but let me explain more. You can't ALWAYS control what happens to you, but you can ALWAYS control how you react to it. Here is something I heard Kirk Franklin say and I repeat often when people complain about their situations: "Two twin boys were raised by an alcoholic father. 1 grew up to be an alcoholic & when asked what happened, he said ' I watched my father'... The other grew up and never drank in his life. When he was asked what happened he said, 'I watched my father'... 2 boys. Same dad. 2 different perspectives. Your perspective in life will determine your destination."

In the book, 'Extreme Ownership,' Jocko Willink talks about how you must own every single thing in your life. When Clay talks about F6 goals, he is talking about owning every single aspect of your life. If you aren't where you want to be or heading where you want to be, it's your fault. I'm going to repeat that line at least 10 times in this chapter and hopefully it will click for you. If you aren't where you want to be or heading where you want to be, it's your fault. When I was younger, I was diagnosed with dyslexia and ADHD, and I used it as a crutch for a long time. I also used to go to a speech pathologist because I couldn't pronounce my R's and people mocked my voice all the time. I've always been motivated person, however, if you told me to do something I would do it but I would find the absolute easiest way to do it.

When I noticed I didn't have to read out loud in class if I complained, I would say I was scared and that it was tough for me. Oh man, did I jump on that bandwagon. I learned that trick young and rode it as far as I could. I wasn't actually scared of reading out loud. I actually liked being the class clown, so if people laughed, it didn't matter as long as I made them laugh. In middle school, I didn't have to take the same tests as other kids. They sent me to a separate room and I got to take special tests.

I understood how playing the victim could get me out of many situations. However, here is what happened: I started to believe it. I started to believe that I wasn't as smart as other kids. I just accepted the fact that I was stupid and it bled over into everything. Everything you tell yourself starts to manifest in your head. So be careful what you think and say about yourself, because you will start to think it's true. For example, as I am writing this book I am struggling with the grammar a lot. Like a lot. It's embarrassing. It's like an 8th grade writing level. That's because I've told myself since I was in 6th grade that I'm terrible at English and writing. I've cheated my way through every English class I've ever been in. In college, I would pay other students for past papers or even just pay them to write a whole paper for me. I accepted the fact that I was bad at writing. In turn, this is a huge reason why I'm writing this book. I hate it, but I've learned immensely while writing it. I know that I need to continue to do things I don't like to help get me to where I want to be. Clay Clark stuttered while he was growing up and was bullied very hard because of that, yet here he is with his business podcast hitting the top of the iTunes charts 6 times, hosting conferences with thousands of people and doing speaking events for massive companies. Clay grew up poor, yet as I write this he has built 13 multimillion dollar companies and written 17 books.

> "Practice, practice, practice in speaking
> before an audience will tend to remove
> all fear of audiences, just as practice
> in swimming will lead to confidence
> and facility in the water. You must
> learn to speak by speaking."

Dale Carnegie

(Dale Carnegie was an American writer and lecturer, and the developer of courses in self-improvement, salesmanship, corporate training, public speaking, and interpersonal skills.)

Jordan Peterson has used this quote in interviews multiple times. In an interview with The Heritage Foundation in particular, he says that the absolute worst thing you can do is tell someone, especially young people, that they are fine the way they are. This cripples them. When you tell someone that they don't really have a choice in the matter, it strips them of their power. Maybe you're a teenager and all your childhood was growing up seeing your alcoholic dad beat you and your mother, so you get to act out in school, bully people, don't study, do drugs, and contemplate suicide. The last thing you need is a sympathetic person telling you, "You're okay the way you are." That's not what you need or want to hear. The truth is, you're currently useless. You have 60 years to put yourself together and God only knows what you could become. Dedicate yourself to continual growth to becoming more than what you currently are. Your current situation and past does not define the rest of your life. Yes, shitty things happen to people, but they happen to all people. It's up to you to dig deep and realize that you can change your current situation and future.

Have you ever said or heard anyone say, "That's just who I am"? My experience has taught me there is no helping these people. You say, "Hey man why are you always late?" And they say, "It's not my fault, that's just who I am." If you have someone like this in your life you need to be very careful and not spend too much time around them. They don't grow or change and they don't believe anyone has a choice in almost anything they do. I was at a conference recently and heard a motivational speaker who is quite possibly the worst speaker I have heard. Nothing made coherent sense. He was not only wrong, but he was the opposite of correct. He's a marriage counselor who made us all sit through a depressive speech. One of the few parts of his speech that I could actually follow was when he said, "You can't control things in your life. And you shouldn't try. People who try to control things in their life have more anxiety than those who don't. You are absolutely fine the way you are." WRONG! Wrong in every single possible way. This speaker was speaking to business owners. If you're a failing business owner and you're about to go bankrupt, do you think the answer to that is? "Don't worry you're fine the way you are. There are outside factors that you can't control." A little bonus nugget, he also said he could fix anyone's problems after the conference for $3,000. What an absolute joke. The business owner that is going bankrupt needs to hear, "It is your fault and that's a good thing because that means you can change what you're doing and grow."

Before I say this next part I want to preface by saying I love my family. They mean the world to me and I always wish the best for them. However, if you want to learn how to make excuses and ignore obvious facts, take time to hang out with my family and they will teach you everything you need to know on that subject. I'll give two examples of my family ignoring obvious facts. I'm going to describe how I tried to talk to them about their weight and finances, and I'll let you find the excuse. When I read 'Rich Dad Poor Dad,' I immediately went and bought 6 copies. I gave 5 to friends and 1 to my parents and said, "This book is incredible and will help you get financial freedom! It actually teaches you to get out of the rat race and get rich! Will y'all please read this for me?" They said, "Absolutely." I came back three months later, and my mom is putting a puzzle together on the computer and my dad is watching Netflix. I ask, "Hey, have you all read 'Rich Dad Poor Dad' yet?" Their response was "No, we don't have time." Did they actually not have time or did they just prioritize Netflix and puzzles over reading the book? I will let you figure out if they were right.

The other one is being overweight. There are multiple interactions I could use, but the main excuses are genetics, not having time to go to the gym, diets are hard to stick to, how hard it is to find food to fit in the diet, deciding to skip breakfast but still not losing weight, so nothing works. Here is what I see: my mom and dad are both overweight. My sister (who, like me, is adopted which matters because then it couldn't be genetic), is very overweight. Both dogs are very overweight, so much so, that they hardly fit through the doggy door. My sister gets McDonalds every single lunch after she is picked up by my Grandma. In the house, there are Little Debbie snack cakes and brownies easily accessible on the counter at all times. My mom gets 2-3 large Diet Dr. Peppers everyday from the gas station.

Everyone who lives in the house is overweight including someone that doesn't have the same genetics. I'll let you decide who's right. I am not using this part of the book as an "I just told you so," for my family. I'm using it because maybe you're making the same or similar excuse for something even though the true reason (your actions) is what's keeping you from your goals.

> » Do you believe you have no control of anything that happens in your life?

> » What have you been blaming others for that you know now is your fault?

> » What excuses are you giving for not bettering yourself?

CHAPTER 6

YOU MUST SAY 'NO' TO GROW

"People think focus means saying yes to the thing you've got to focus on. But that's not what it means at all. It means saying no to the hundred other good ideas that there are. You have to pick carefully. I'm actually as proud of the things we haven't done as the things I have done. Innovation is saying no to 1,000 things."

Steve Jobs

(Co-founder of Apple, the founder of NeXT and the former CEO of Pixar)

"A person's success in life can usually be measured by the number of uncomfortable conversations he or she is willing to have."

Tim Ferriss

(Bestselling author of The 4-Hour Work Week, venture capitalist and podcaster)

I'm going to keep this chapter short. It's something most of the world struggles with because they have FOMO (Fear Of Missing Out) or they are scared to hurt feelings. However, it's simple so I'm not going to over complicate it. I've seen Clay say no way more than I've seen him say yes. His time is very valuable, so he chooses carefully how to spend it. He is constantly offered new business ideas or partnerships and asked to go to dinner. He simply says no. Not in a mean way, but in a respectful and professional way. If it does not align with his F6 goals, he simply says no. You have to determine what's important to you and schedule it.

In Chapter 3, we talked about making a calendar. You should now have a schedule laid out that will help you reach your goals. The key is simply to not let others add to your schedule or to-do list. For example, Clay said this in his ThriveTime Show podcast titled 'How to Design a Sustainable Schedule' Clay said, "I have just finished putting together a book and you can get it from your business coach and I will help you. I think it's on Amazon now, it's called, *The Art of Getting Things Done.*" In this book I teach you there are many, many moves that you can use. I talked to Dr. Z about some of these moves. Some of these moves you might go, 'that's a really dirty move'. But this is an example: If somebody calls you, you don't have to call them back. You don't have to, so you have to ask yourself, 'Is this relationship one that I want to maintain?' So, just as an example, if you email me, I don't have to email back, because I get thousands of emails. Just because you emailed me doesn't mean you can put something on my to-do list. Make sure that you're getting this idea. Just because somebody emailed me, it doesn't mean they just one-upped me on the organizational chart. Just because you sent me an email does not mean you have the right to take a minute of my day."

Don't let other people control your schedule. I watch Clay go into meetings or interviews and he leaves his phone outside of the room. If you spend your whole day being reactive to things you will never get anything done. It is okay to tell people no. For example, when I first moved out to Nashville I agreed to play basketball on Wednesday mornings 6 - 8 a.m.. I did that for about a month and a half. I got busier with the business so I needed that time back for the business. I had to have that conversation with my friend that I won't be playing anymore. Even though I made that commitment, I had to replace it. I told him when I get the business to a spot where it can run without me then I'll start playing again.

Here is another controversial thing Clay does, when he gets home, he turns his phone off. He is completely unreachable. He will be constantly bombarded with employee issues, employee wins, burning fires, issues with speakers on the tours, and many other things he doesn't care about at that moment.

Clay is one of the few people I've ever heard of that is as busy as he is and yet, his wife and family still loves him. Which even if you're not super busy, unfortunately that is a rare thing now a days. That's because they sat down and had that conversation and he has scheduled family nights and date nights. During that time it's dedicated to just family and/or his wife Vanessa. He isn't bringing work home with him or running back to the office because of people calling him with "emergencies".

I want you to give yourself permission to say no. It's okay to say no to dinners, meetings, emails, texts or voicemails, Instagram messages, fantasy football, political conversations, or birthday parties. Many people feel bad saying "no, but each time you say 'no' to something that is a waste of time, it's saying 'yes' to bettering your future. Not only do you have to say 'no' to other people you need to start saying 'no' to yourself. Stop spending time on Facebook, Instagram, Netflix, or Xbox. If you want to be successful, you need to start trading in Netflix for reading. You must start trading in things that waste time for things that better your future. If you're honest with yourself, you know what those are.

If you've made it to this part of the book, you're serious about bettering yourself. I've found that most people who are serious about changing their life already know what's bad for them and what they should be doing. Earlier in this book I talked to you about the Jordan Peterson Challenge. If you have done that then you know what you're currently doing that you shouldn't be doing. You need to combine saying 'no' to those things and trading up for things you should be doing. Schedule time on your calendar to do those things.

**HERE ARE 5 SUPER MOVES
FROM CLAY'S BOOK THE ART
OF GETTING THINGS DONE.**

» Cut negative team members and family members out of your life.

» Get your email inbox to zero during the morning and stop checking it incessantly during the day.

» Stop arguing about politics.

» Stop arguing about religion.

» Stop focusing on what you cannot control.

In the rest of the book, he has 66 super moves of getting things done.

"We all work hard. We're all as busy as can be. When it doesn't seem like we could possibly get any busier, we do. But if you're not focused on the right things, you'll be the busiest guy in the poor house. You have to focus on the right things in the right order, and you have to tolerate a lack of perfection. There will always be more tasks than time and more decisions than data. Your task is to determine what's really important: what do you have to do and do well? The challenge is the same whether you are running a startup or a multi-million dollar company that's been around for thirty-five years."

 Jim McCann

(The founder of 1800Flowers.com)

The whole point of this chapter is this: You need to say 'no' to the things that steal time so you can say 'yes' to things that maximize your time. I'm going to end this chapter with a wake-up call about your smartphone. These are some articles that will hopefully bring light to why you need to cut social media out and get your time back.

86% of Americans say they check their email and social media accounts "constantly," and that it's really stressing them out.

https://www.businessinsider.com/what-your-smartphone-is-doing-to-your-brain-and-it-isnt-good-2018-3

Twice as many heavy users of electronic devices are unhappy, depressed, or distressed as light users.

https://time.com/5555737/smartphone-mental-health-teens/

Endocrinologist Robert Lustig tells Business Insider that notifications from our phones are training our brains to be in a near constant state of stress and fear by establishing a stress-fear memory pathway. Such a state means that the prefrontal cortex, the part of our brains that normally deals with some of our highest-order cognitive functioning, goes completely haywire, and basically shuts down.

https://www.businessinsider.com/what-your-smartphone-is-doing-to-your-brain-and-it-isnt-good-2018-3

Checking Facebook has been proven to make young adults depressed. Researchers who've studied college students' emotional well-being find a direct link: the more often people check Facebook, the more miserable they are. But the incessant, misery-inducing phone checking doesn't just stop there. Games like Fortnite or apps like Twitter can be addictive, in the sense that they will leave your brain craving another hit.

https://www.businessinsider.com/what-your-smartphone-is-doing-to-your-brain-and-it-isnt-good-2018-3

Nielson average person spends an average of 11.3 hours per day consuming media on their smartphone.

https://www.inc.com/melanie-curtin/are-you-on-your-phone-too-much-average-person-spends-this-many-hours-on-it-every-day.html

There is a concerning relationship between excessive screen time and risk for death by suicide, depression, suicidal ideation and suicidal attempts,

https://news.fsu.edu/news/health-medicine/2017/11/30/fsu-researcher-finds-link-excessive-screen-time-suicide-risk/

All of these quotes can be found in Clay Clark's book 'Trade Ups.' If I haven't convinced you yet to stop using social media and your phone, then you need to go read his full book on the subject.

Out of all the sections in this book, this is going to be the most controversial one. If you're a keyboard warrior and haven't made a post about how bad this book is, you're about to. There are people who you know that are always having a bad day. No matter what is going on, they have something to complain about. At first they seem so sensitive, thoughtful, and caring. Then you get drawn in and you realize they are sensitive, but they are too sensitive and it only goes inward. They take things very personally. Sometimes it's small stuff like their order got messed up at the fast food restaurant or they had someone honk at them in traffic. But whatever is wrong in their day, it's never their fault, it's always someone else's. Things that you would typically just brush off, they will hold on to for weeks. Then it turns into bigger things like they had an abusive dad or some traumatic story with an ex, their cousins best friend knew a guy that died, etc. By this point, you've already been sucked in so you console them and you give them more attention. This is exactly what they seek. They learned from an early age that they receive more attention when they are sad than when they are happy. These people are what I call dream killers. You will bring up a victory you recently had like you got a new job or a personal record, and somehow they turn it around and now you're consoling them on something else. You start downplaying your life, you stop striving, and you stop wanting more. People like this will suck the soul from you. These people

are often family members or friends. You must cut these people out of your life. It's not mean. It's a necessity. Do not shrink because other people are not succeeding around you. If you feel this way read the quote below.

> "Our deepest fear is not that we are inadequate. Our deepest fear is that we are powerful beyond measure. It is our light, not our darkness that most frightens us. We ask ourselves, 'Who am I to be brilliant, gorgeous, talented, fabulous?' Actually, who are you not to be? You are a child of God. Your playing small does not serve the world. There is nothing enlightened about shrinking so that other people won't feel insecure around you. We are all meant to shine, as children do. We were born to make manifest the glory of God that is within us. It's not just in some of us; it's in everyone. And as we let our own light shine, we unconsciously give other people permission to do the same. As we are liberated from our own fear, our presence automatically liberates others."

 Marianne Williamson

(Marianne Deborah Williamson is an American author, speaker, humanitarian, and presidential candidate.)

You must cut these people out of your lives. You must say 'no' to these people. You need to surround yourself with people who will push and motivate you not pull you down. Don't try to be the hero that is pulling everyone up. You know why people always complain about people changing when they become successful? Because if they never changed, they wouldn't have become successful. When you start being successful, it's because you've had to change. You've had to start saying no to people, family, movies, sleeping in, video games, social media, flag football leagues, unscheduled days, instant gratification, and much more. If you start saying 'no' more than you say 'yes', you'll start to be successful. People will say you've changed, but you need to know and remember that's a good thing.

Clay says when you get to the top of success you'll find that there aren't a whole lot of people up there. Very few people wake up at 3 a.m. or 4 a.m. every day. When you wake up at 3 a.m. or 4 a.m. every day it becomes a habit and you are already significantly ahead of the average person because they don't want to wake up. Most people aim for small hills, but you're aiming for a mountain top. So not only do you already have a competitive edge because you wake up early, you are also aiming higher than them even your failure is higher than their success. What happens is the people who remember you from high school start saying " Who does he think he is, on top of Mt. Money?" They start throwing rocks at you because they're not alone.

It's like a mob mentality. Instead of asking you how to get there or asking for help, they just throw rocks out of spite. They go on social media or see you in public and they throw their rocks.

Everyone wants a cheat code, so my only cheat code for you that I have found so far is that the easiest way to change your life is to surround yourself with people who are people you want to be like. Whether you're willing to admit it or not, you are a product of your environment. Don't try to be great while simultaneously surrounding yourself with fools. My friend, I am excited for you to embark on this journey.

POST CHAPTER QUESTIONS

> » What activities are you currently participating in that you know you need to say 'no' to?

> » Who are the emotionally draining people who you need to stop spending time with?

> » What changes do you need to make in route to becoming successful?

CHAPTER 7
WHAT'S NEXT

You made it to the end of the book. Congratulations! Unless you just flipped to the last chapter to skim, CHEATER! After you read this book you're going to have three possible outcomes. They are listed below. If you ever feel unmotivated or it gets hard, come back to this chapter and read them.

Option one: You choose to implement nothing from this book. Life goes back to normal and nothing changes. You continue to drift through life with no actual action plan on how to reach your goal. Maybe you don't even set goals. You don't have the mental fortitude it takes to simply do the work to set the goals. Most people fall into this category simply because they don't know any different. However, you read this book, so now you know better. If you personally fall into this category, have fun. You won't magically drift into success, but it is possible to drift into living in the van down by the river.

Option two: You have the mental fortitude to start your journey to success. You write out your F6 goals on a whiteboard. You make your calendar and you make your schedule. You start saying no and cutting out unproductive activities while replacing them with productive ones. You are highly motivated and feel highly dedicated. Unfortunately, after a week or two, the alarm clock continues going off early and your friends start getting upset because you've "changed." That little voice in your head starts to creep in. It's telling you there's no need to get up early, why bother writing it down and having a clipboard if your phone is always with you anyway? You start to make excuses on why these things don't actually apply to you. You say things like, "If I had a schedule like them, I'd make a calendar," or, "starting the day at 9 a.m. is still early and serves the same purpose as waking up at 4 or 5 a.m.." Now you've hit the wall where everything is in place, but the initial motivation to be great has faded away. That voice is in control. You have implemented half of your goals, but even the stuff you implement you only do halfway. You start drifting into being like everyone else again.

Option three: Only a select few make it. Everything starts the same as option two. You have the mental fortitude to start your journey to success. You write out your F6 goals on a white board. You make your calendar and you make your schedule. You start saying 'no' and cutting out unproductive activities and replacing them with productive ones. You are highly motivated and feel highly dedicated. However, after a week or two, the alarm clock goes off early and friends start getting upset because

you've "changed" and you don't make time for them anymore. That little voice in your head starts to come in. It's telling you there's no need to get up early, why write it down and have a clipboard if your phone is always with you anyways. Fortunately, you understand that what's scheduled gets done. You understand why you started. You understand you want to have time and financial freedom. You understand: "You want to live like no one else, so later you can live like no one else" (Dave Ramsey). So you go to the mirror and look yourself in the eye, and you tell the voice to shut the hell up, you got stuff to do.

My friend, Clay and I understand everyone has the ability to be great. That's why his goal is to mentor millions and that's why I wrote this book. The reality is that most just don't have the fortitude to bore down and have a magnificent obsession with being great. Do you?

BONUS CHAPTER

SUPER MOVES OFTEN USED TO GUARANTEE FAILURE

HOW TO BE SUPER UNSUCCESSFUL

"Failure isn't fatal, but failure
to change might be."

John Wooden

(John Robert Wooden was an American basketball coach
and player. Nicknamed the "Wizard of Westwood", he
won ten National Collegiate Athletic Association national
championships in a 12-year period as head coach for the
UCLA Bruins, including a record seven in a row.)

Clay's evil twin, Claytron Menedez, wrote a book called, 'How to Repel Potential Friends and Not Influence People.' I want to walk you through a day in the life of Clayton Menedez. Claytron Mendez is the epitome of what happens in the life of an unsuccessful person.

Claytron starts his day by hitting snooze on his alarm clock that he often forgets to even set. He rolls back over under the covers to get the 5 extra minutes of sleep that, obviously, are going to make him feel well rested after a long night of drinking and hanging out with people he doesn't even like. He finally wakes up. Now he has no time to shower. The next thing he does is check his phone and goes on Social Media. He sees calls and texts from his boss asking him where he is. Claytron doesn't write anything down. He solely operates off of memorizing everything and keeping it in his head. He doesn't schedule anything in the calendar, so he forgot the sales proposal deadline was this morning at 10 a.m. They set it at 10 so he would have plenty of time to get it turned in. His boss calls, and Claytron says, "The proposal is done and I'm on my way into the office." (This is a lie.) Then Claytron's boss fires him.

Claytron is overjoyed because Claytron hated that job anyways, it was too stressful. Claytron gets a call from a friend to go to lunch. Even though he hates this friend, he says 'yes' anyways. They go to lunch. Claytron shows up late and then blames traffic even though he didn't leave until the time he was supposed to be there. Claytron tells his friend he got fired because he feels the management doesn't understand him and he wasn't treated fairly anyways. He decides to leave a review saying how bad it is to work there. They proceed to argue about politics and religion. Claytron knows he is always correct so if he disagrees with someone he doesn't let them finish their thought and immediately cuts them off to tell them his point of view.

After they finish their two hour lunch, Claytron decides that he is motivated to work out because he has more time.

Claytron then goes to the gym to work out. Halfway there, he remembers he has a bowling league that night, so he doesn't want to be sore for it. He decides he will just spend time in the hot tub at the gym and not work out. While in the hot tub, Claytron scrolls through social media the whole time and responds to comments on his post and other people's comments. He gets into an argument over abortion on social media and multiple people disagree with him. Claytron starts to get stressed out and starts feeling depressed because the people on his phone screen (that he can control if he looks at or not) called him mean names.

Claytron Mendez goes back home to his room in his mom's house. He starts doing research on unemployment benefits, and realizes he can make between $400 and $450 a week from unemployment. He thinks that's great because he lives at home and has no real expenses anyway. He asks his mom to set up his unemployment benefits for him. His mom asks him when he is moving out, seeing as he is already 42 years old. He starts yelling at her saying, " You don't even love me mom! Jimmy's mom never treats him like this. I don't even get an allowance and I have to do these dishes once a week. The least you can do is set this up for me. I'll move out when I'm ready, but this is my safe place and I haven't been able to find another safe place anywhere. I could go back to college, but you know they don't understand how I learn."

Claytron decides to binge his favorite TV show on Netflix. Once he gets done with that, he plays Xbox until about 2 a.m. He is about to go to bed, but realizes he doesn't have to be up because he doesn't have a job anymore. He decides to watch videos on things he doesn't like so he can comment on them and tell people he doesn't like the videos.

The truth is Claytron is a fictional character, but real people live like Claytron. Don't be a Claytron, and cut the Claytrons out of your life.

"People change, seldom."

Dr. Robert Zollner

(Doctor Robert H. Zoellner has been a successful optometrist and entrepreneur within the city of Tulsa for over 22 years. However, most would consider him to be an entrepreneur first and an optometrist 2nd, 3rd, 4th, or 5th. As a self-made millionaire, who started his career with nothing but passionate diligence.)

"The time will never be just right, you must act now."

Napoleon Hill

(Best-selling author of "Think and Grow Rich.)

Printed in the USA
CPSIA information can be obtained
at www.ICGtesting.com
LVHW030718310124
770461LV00074B/2598